BENEATH THE SURFACE

Beneath the Surface

The Wildlife Art of David Miller

LANGFORD PRESS · 2007

To Lisa, Jenny and Thomas. Martin and Kate

Langford Press, 10 New Road, Langtoft
Peterborough PE6 9LE
www.langford-press.co.uk
Email sales@langford-press.co.uk

Designed and typeset in Cycles and Magma
by Nye Hughes, Dalrymple, Edinburgh
Printed in Singapore under the supervision
of MRM Graphics Ltd, Winslow
Photography by Mike Roberts, Electra Studios,
Port Talbot

A CIP record for this book is available
from the British Library
ISBN 978-1-904078-25-8

Illustrated opposite title page:
Sand Eel Shoal, oil on board, 12 × 8 inches

www.davidmillerart.co.uk

Preface

When Ian Langford first telephoned to ask if I was interested in producing a book of my fish paintings, my initial delight quickly turned to panic. My mind ran riot with thoughts of the pictures I have yet to paint and of how I couldn't possibly have enough fish pictures to fill a book. Producing a mock-up soon calmed me down, as did Ian's encouragement and the realisation that 'Beneath the Surface' is only the story of my fish paintings to date; hopefully there will be more to come. The book consists mainly of work produced over the last five years, and I don't think it is any coincidence that this is exactly the length of time I have been diving. I have been a professional artist for almost twenty years, but in that time, despite the fact that I am often referred to as 'the fish man', I have also produced many paintings of birds, mammals and landscapes. I sometimes feel, especially in these days where unmade beds and lights going on and off win the art prizes, that painting wildlife in a realistic style might be considered anachronistic, but I know that despite such feelings I shall continue to work in this way. Perhaps I am a simple soul, but I think that there is, and always will be, value and legitimacy in an artist responding to the natural world with the painting of a picture. I know from the response to my paintings, and the success of contemporary wildlife art generally, that there is a place for such work. The simple fact that I am often told by customers how much pleasure my art brings them gives me the confidence to feel that my paintings have a relevance and are worth the effort and energy that go into their production.

With regards to the text in this, my first book and my first serious attempt at writing for over twenty years, I wasn't sure where to begin at first. I started off by accompanying the pictures with rather dry facts about the species portrayed but quickly realised that this wasn't working, and for the first time I started to question why I was painting fish in the first place. This led me to explore the intensity of my early life as an angler when, from the age of ten through to my early twenties, I was simply obsessed with the sport. In the book I have tried to capture the enthusiasm of those early years, for it was this period that set fish swimming through my imagination. By diving and snorkelling over the last twenty years, I have revisited my childhood imagination, using my work as an artist to translate this into paint.

DAVID MILLER ST CLEARS, 2007

THE KELP FOREST
[detail] · oil on board · 8 x 12 inches

Acknowledgements

I would have been unable to continue working as an artist or prepare this book without the help and encouragement of many people. Firstly my gratitude goes to Ian Langford for offering me the opportunity to add to the titles in his excellent Wildlife Art Series, which has done a fantastic job in championing contemporary wildlife art. I need to thank my parents for teaching me the value of hard work, without which I think it is impossible to succeed as an artist.

Of the good friends who have helped me in many ways I am indebted most of all to Martin and Kate Savage, as without their continued moral and practical support over the past fifteen years I wouldn't be working as a full-time artist. A fellow artist and constant friend since college, who has inspired me by his example and offered practical advice on all matters of fieldwork, painting and making a living from art, is Martin Ridley. In recent years in Wales two other artists, David Cowdry and Andrew Evans, have helped to keep me sane through their fantastic friendship and their ability to withstand many of my worst excesses as a blatherskite.

Also in Wales, I am indebted to Tony and Connie Bate, whose generosity encouraged my painting as a college leaver and in recent years gave me a place to work and thrive when it was most needed.

From my angling days my warmest gratitude goes to Jack Hayes, who not only taught me to fish but also encouraged my early efforts with pencil and brush. For angling companionship I would like to thank Mark Minshull, Paddy McDermott and Clive Mingham. I also need to thank Paddy for leading by example and ensuring that during this book project my mind has stayed focused on the job at hand. My thanks also go to Robin Armstrong for his generous foreword, and to all the other artists whose work has inspired me. Thanks also to Merlin Unwin Publishers for their permission to use the excerpt from *An Angler for All Seasons* by H.T. Sheringham (ISBN 9781 873674 04 8), in the Tench section of this book and to Faber and Faber for the use of two poems by Ted Hughes.

I feel that these acknowledgements could take over the whole book as I have benefited so much from the kindness of others, including Brian and Val Warren, Keith and Mary Hutchins, Pat Cunningham, Richard Afflick, Jean Gale and Joan Frost of the Millyard Gallery and Graham Jones of Planet Prints.

Finally, my deepest gratitude goes to my wife Lisa, for her love and encouragement over many years. Without Lisa there would certainly be no book and not nearly so many paintings, and I know that I would have been forced to get a 'proper job' but for her hard work and determination.

Foreword

My own early interest in painting fishes began innocently enough on one of my many teenage visits to the Natural History Museum in South Kensington, where I would go to draw and paint the many and varied exhibits on display. On one such visit I wandered into the souvenir shop and there in one of the print browsers I saw a picture of a little brown trout, resplendent with black and red spots and idling beside some water crowfoot in a clear stream. The artist was that master of English countryside art, Charles Tunnicliffe. I was so impressed by this picture that from then on I included fish in my repertoire.

Later on, when, like many young hopefuls, I took my portfolio with considerable trepidation to one of the big sporting and wildlife galleries for some appraisal, I was told in no uncertain terms that paintings of fish were not saleable. The advice I was given was to stick to birds and mammals. I chose to ignore this advice and I'm very glad I did, because otherwise we may not have had the opportunity to enjoy this wonderful collection of new paintings by David Miller.

When I met David for the first time he told me that whilst at art college his passion for painting fish had been inspired by the work that I had been producing, and that without reference to it he may well not have pursued this very demanding subject further!

The first painting I saw by David was in a little gallery in Stockbridge, epicentre for chalk-stream fishing in Europe and possibly the world. Coincidentally it was a picture of a brown trout, idling in the stream, garlands of weed waving gently beside it and yes, you've guessed it, some strands of water crowfoot sitting on the surface to complete the picture. Quintessentially English maybe, but, believe me, David Miller's passion goes much deeper than that, quite literally.

He took up diving for the sole purpose of seeing his subjects at first hand in their own special environment, firstly in the rivers, lakes and streams around where he used to live and latterly in the coastal waters of Wales, where he now resides. These experiences, coupled, I'm sure, with the obvious sights involved, have breathed new life into his current body of work. Evocative paintings of marauding bass searing into shoals of sand eels with greats masses of saline bubbles crashing down from the surf and swell above. For an angler, this scene can only be imagined from the rocks or a dingy above, but look into one of David Miller's paintings and the whole scene is revealed before your very eyes! Contrasting with this, imagine some gnarled dark tree root hidden beneath the murky waters of a private lake that no one has fished for fifty years. There camouflaged and concealed you can just make out the outline of a monster pike, maybe 40lbs or more! In the foreground and temptingly close is a shoal of small rudd or roach. Will the great *Esox* lunge at the roach or will he wait until you, the angler from above, are ready to lower your small dead mackerel bait into a position to lure him from his hideaway.

Above the surface we look into a trout pool, at first we see only the bank-side vegetation and possibly a mayfly or two, then peering a little harder we can just, but only just, make out the outline of a 5lb brown trout – will he rise? If he does, will it be to one of the naturals in the picture or will your feather replica appear from outside the frame and be engulfed. This is what David's painting is all about, presenting to the viewer that 'magic moment'. Most of the scenes that David paints are virtually unphotographable, and even if they weren't I know that he would use the resultant image only as an aide-mémoire. His paintings are no slavish workings from snapshots taken on a scuba-diving trip, they are carefully constructed and composed and they reveal to us all the passion that he feels for his chosen subject.

I have exhibited alongside David and can honestly say that it is a delight in this new world of aggressive competition to meet an artist whose mild-mannered ways, modesty and love of his young family take priority.

Come with me then 'Beneath the Surface' to enjoy the world below with a young painter who has yet to reach forty and whose work I know will continue to go from strength to strength.

The Langford Press have achieved a great deal in championing published wildlife art in this country and in this marvellous new book by David Miller have added another gem to the valuable collection.

ROBIN ARMSTRONG LOPWELL, 2007

Introduction

I cannot remember a time when I wasn't transfixed by some aspect of the natural world. I grew up amongst the most unpromising, at least from a naturalist's point of view, dreary mill terraces of Oldham; yet even here the sparrows nesting under the guttering, the kestrels perched on the chimneys ready to ambush them and the swifts screaming on a summer's evening were enough to fire my enthusiasm. Added to this were the delights of weekends spent on my grandparents' dairy farm on what was left of the town's rural fringe. Here in the old stone shippen and in the hay loft that could have been lifted straight from an Andrew Wyeth painting, I could marvel at the swallows' aerobatics and peer into their nests. Amongst the rougher areas of pasture, with a soundtrack of 'Peeoo-wit, peeoo-wit', I used to look for lapwings' nests and gaze in wonder at the perfection of their speckled eggs and impossibly cute chicks. I also discovered my first badger sett and somewhat naively spent an afternoon in waiting, hoping that one might make an appearance.

Through books and TV natural history programmes, my interest extended to more exotic places and species, and I spent hours of my childhood copying from encyclopaedias such delights as the Philippino monkey-eating eagle, great white shark, tiger, Tyrannosaurus rex and dimetrodon. My interest was in every aspect of natural history and the title of this book may well have related to birds or mammals if it hadn't been for a couple of incidents which, around the age of ten, turned me into a passionate angler.

The first was at Alexandra Park Boating Lake during one of the long hot summers of childhood and involved the shoals of sticklebacks that lived there. One day, armed with a net and an empty sweet jar purloined from the local corner shop, still lives bright in my memory. Fish after fish rewarded my patience by the lakeside: silver-bellied, armour-plated sticklebacks, the occasional breeding male as red as red can be. They seemed almost too perfect to have been plucked from the unpromising, green-tinged, litter-strewn boating lake, and I knew immediately that feeling familiar to all fishermen – 'just one more, just one more'. Long after my companions had grown bored and wandered off to find some new distraction, I remained, despite sunburnt calves and a growling stomach. I did eventually march home in triumph with the day's prize to show them off to anybody who showed even a little interest (and indeed to anybody who didn't!). Finding them all dead in the morning took the edge off my joy and I learned in future to return my catch.

The second was on the pond that nestled in the corner of the biggest field on my grandparents' farm. For us youngsters the farm-pond, rumoured to be virtually bottomless as it lay over old mine-workings, was out of bounds, so of course we visited it regularly, sneaking down the blind side of the hedgerow to avoid discovery. Once there we would do all the usual things that small boys do at ponds – throwing in stones, poking around with sticks, flooding our wellies and being told off by fishermen. These earnest and usually old men sat transfixed

Early success – a carp from Tanner's Dam

by something on the water's surface and I felt somehow drawn to them. A strange excitement and sense of possibility seemed to pervade their stillness, and if you waited long enough a sudden flurry of activity would occur after what seemed hours of inertia. Then the prize was brought to hand. My first close encounter was with a roach, so silver-bright and scale perfect that I doubt I could have been more impressed if the angler had been an alchemist and had turned the pond-side mud to gold before my nine-year-old eyes. I had to perform that same magic and begged my parents for fishing tackle the following Christmas. This duly arrived in the form of a white, solid glass rod with bright red whippings and an Intrepid Boyo fixed-spool reel. I felt sick with excitement even as I tackled up amongst the Christmas chaos of the living room. I then needed help, as nobody in my close family went fishing. I stumbled along for a while, making clumsy efforts with a couple of friends, gleaning what I could from books, before two neighbours intervened.

The first, Jack Hayes, was a man of my parents' age and an angler with years of experience. Jack took me under his wing, enrolling me as a junior member of his local club and, with much kindness and patience, taught me how to fish. Whenever I fished with Jack he put my success before his own, patiently untangling my birds' nests (and there were many!), rescuing my float from bank-side trees after yet another misplaced cast and, most importantly, bringing fish to my hand and therefore building my confidence. On one of my early trips with Jack I caught, at least for a small boy, a mind-boggling roach of a pound and a quarter, which in context is still one of the most impressive fish I have seen in thirty years of angling. Jack also encouraged my earliest efforts at drawing and painting fish and still has one or two of my early originals hanging in his home.

The second neighbour was Martin Savage, who was in the same year as my elder brother at primary school. Martin introduced me to waters that I could reach on the local bus routes, such as Tanner's Dam, the Huddersfield Narrow Canal and the River Tame, places where I would go on to spend half my adolescence. He also introduced me to poaching the very first time he took me on the River Tame in Saddleworth. He seemed to gloss over my questions about permits, as I could clearly see the S.A.D.A.S. 'Private Fishing' signs everywhere and was a little worried. We hadn't been fishing above an hour when he shouted 'Quick, Beardie's here, run for it!' A bearded giant of a man, reminiscent of a Viking warrior, and an equally large Alsatian, which could have doubled for the Hound of the Baskervilles, were soon in hot pursuit. Thankfully we had the river between us and, with the extra speed a surge of adrenalin provides, we escaped to fish another day. I fished with Martin for the next five years until he went to study agriculture in Hampshire, a move which proved vital to my paintings in years to come. I fished with lots of other friends, most of who came and went, but others who became equally obsessed were the McDermott brothers, Paddy and Shaun, and Mark (Mini) Minshull.

Throughout my subsequent development as an angler my mind became filled with images of fish. These images came from fish I had caught myself and from photographs and book illustrations. I soon began copying pictures from the fishing books I had started to collect, which included works by Keith Linsell, Rod Sutterby, Dr Dietrich Burber and the inimitable Bernard Venables.

Angling books were very important to me, and I fished for exotic species in far-away places as often in my imagination as I fished for roach, perch and gudgeon in my local waters. A favourite Christmas present each year was the *Anglers Mail* annual, and over a couple of years I collected a part-work called the *Fisherman's Handbook*. The highlight of each week was its delivery with the morning newspaper, and I can still bring to mind the smell of the printed paper and the excitement on receiving the binders, into which I would lovingly file away each issue until I had completed all three volumes. Other favourites

COARSE FISH

Coarse Fish

For many years I was a dyed-in-the-wool coarse angler, with family holidays providing a brief, usually unsuccessful, flirtation with the sea. Game fishing, especially with the fly, seemed like a mystical dark art and if we saw anybody fly-fishing on the River Tame we would laugh at the ridiculous thickness of their line. During the dullness of school, when the will to live was challenged by such horrors as double chemistry, having a fishing trip on the horizon kept me sane, and a sense of anticipation would build as the weekend approached. All the covers and margins of my school books were filled with doodles of fish and fishing tackle, and many a well-aimed piece of chalk was needed to bring me back to the world of the Periodic Table.

The sense of escape offered by fishing was reinforced later when, during college vacations, I used to work in dark, noisy factories where they always seemed to have special clocks on which a minute lasted an hour, and a weekend's fishing would sustain me through the worst of the week's plastic extrusion. For a whole decade, coarse fishing completely dominated my life and I would get as much pleasure from fishing in my imagination as on the riverbank. Fishing time was also extended by preparation at home, whether it was repairing tackle, making floats, spooling on fresh line, spinning pike traces, stewing hemp or rolling boilies. The last two jobs meant taking over the kitchen of my long-suffering mum, who had already taken some convincing to finally allow me to keep maggots in the family fridge. To this day she is unaware that I once suffered an escape when half a pint of maggots finished up inside a bag of prime sausages. I didn't dare tell her so I simply picked out the escapees, thoroughly washed the sausages, and returned them to the fridge. I didn't enjoy the bangers and mash as usual that night as I couldn't forget the sight of those sausages crawling with maggots; thankfully, the other members of the family ate their meal in blissful ignorance. Everybody survived and my only defence is the fact that I was just twelve and thought that being able to continue using the fridge to store bait was more important than coming clean!

From my mid-twenties I drifted more into game fishing, although I still love to coarse fish, especially for pike. I also love taking my son Tom to fish for roach and rudd, re-living the simple delight in watching a float, bringing a succession of small fish to hand, admiring their beauty and slipping them gently back into the water. Even though I rarely fish now, knowing that it is always there as an option still brings me solace, especially if life seems difficult or work overbearing. I still sometimes promise myself a trip out at the weekend, and even if I don't actually make it, the thought of going fishing has helped me through many an onerous commission or looming deadline.

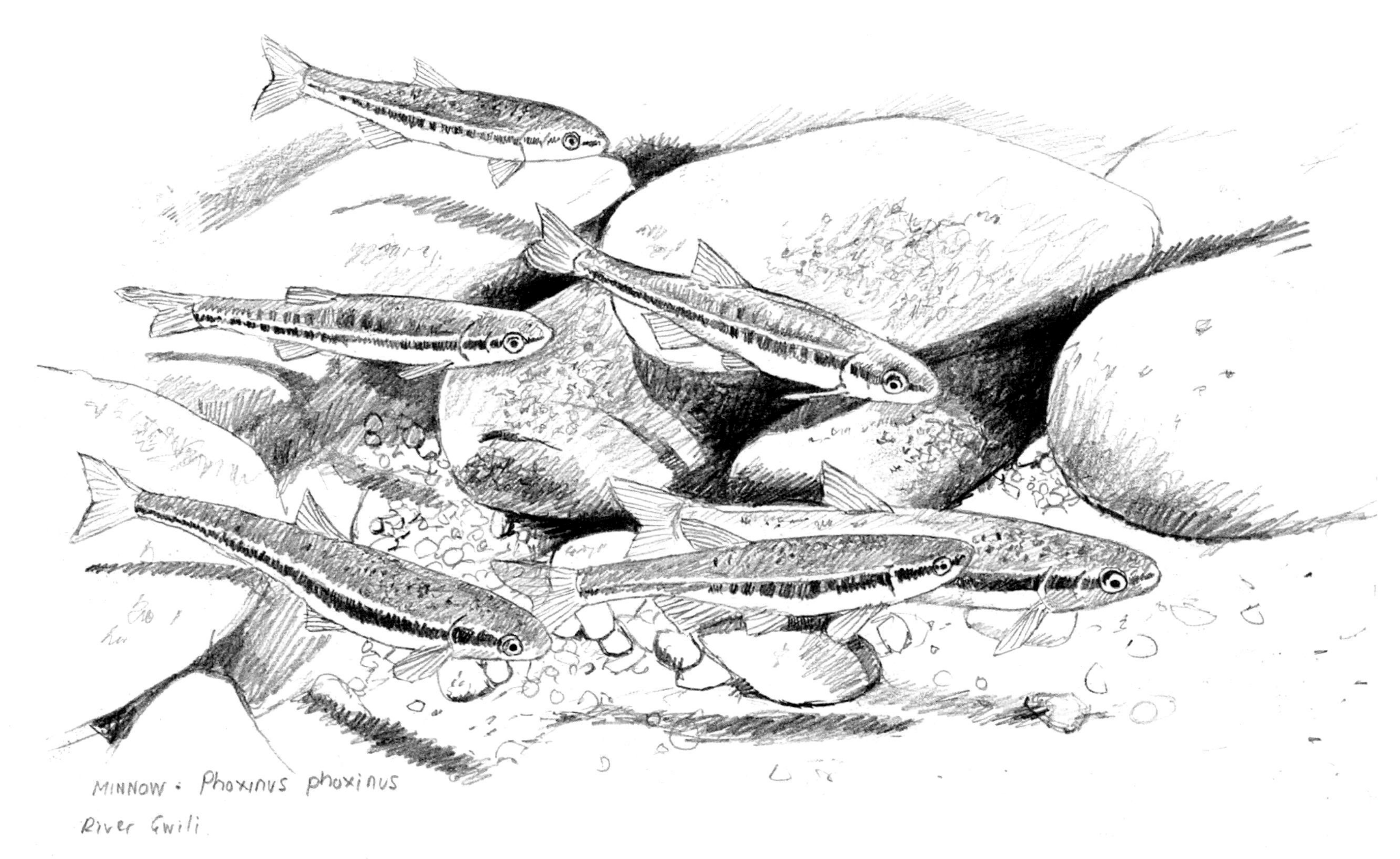

MINNOWS

Graphite on paper · 8 x 11 inches

I often have minnows for company on my dives in pursuit of bigger fish, fussing around to take advantage of any food that might be disturbed by my activities. In the days when I used to snorkel just in my trunks there were some rivers where vast shoals of them would drive me mad, almost inflicting death by tickling, as they would nibble at my bare feet. Whenever I see them, they remind me of the River Tame, for on days when the trout or grayling were difficult, usually when the river ran low and clear, we would hold 'minnow matches'. These worked on the simple basis that we scored one point for a minnow, ten for a trout and fifteen for a grayling. One memorable triumph was in a match against my friend 'Mini', when, with seconds to go and Mini just beginning to stake his claim as the next Ivan Marks because of his ten-point lead, I hooked a grayling, the first we had seen all day, and stole the match.

Rudd, Scardinius erythrophthalmus
These little beauties caught from a small pond in Upper Clatford, Hampshire, and kept briefly in a tank to study for 'Pike & Rudd'.
Chunkier than the roach, with the upturned mouth giving a sligh
bulldog expression.
DAVID MILLER 2006

DAVID MILLER · 2006.
DACE Leuciscus leuciscus.
caught on breadflake from
the R. Anton, Upper Clatford.
Like many fish I've
caught & put in tanks
this dace continued
to try & feed, mouthing
particles in the water.
Like all silver fish in
good condition, this dace
a joy to behold - that 'freshly
minted' look.

Perch

I have to start with perch for, like countless small boys, they were the first fish I caught regularly. Along with gudgeon, small perch were the only fish daft enough to fall for my clumsy methods. Perch and rain go together in my memory, and even without the protection of a fishing brolly I used to sit for hours in the pouring rain in my bright yellow cagoule, just for the thrill of catching one more three-inch perch to add to my day's tally. I caught and saw so many small perch that when I first encountered one of any size it looked almost like a different species. It was rough to the hand, heavily built and fiercely spiked, almost prehistoric somehow, its large dorsal fin reminiscent of the dimetrodon I was always drawing. It certainly brought to mind Richard Walker's quote: 'A big perch is the biggest fish of them all.'

In more recent years some of the best perch fishing I have enjoyed has been on Malham Tarn in Yorkshire, where fish after fish of between ¾lb and 1lb have come to the boat. Splendid handsome fish with clear dark stripes against yellow flanks, with pelvic fins dipped in vermillion. I have had some good encounters here underwater too, with great shoals of perch coming to stare at my intrusion. Perch are often the first fish to appear on a dive, bristling up with a 'what's in it for us' attitude. My most frustrating experience with a camera underwater was with perch. I was photographing small rudd in a gravel pit and had just finished a roll of film when two big perch came barging in within a couple of feet of me before starting to attack the rudd. I immediately got out and loaded up more film but on my return the perch had vanished. These days the wonders of digital photography have cancelled out such problems, and it is fantastic to start a dive not only with 500 shots available but also with the ability to edit as you go. I have only been diving for a year with a good-quality SLR digital camera so there has been a lot of catching up to do after years spent struggling with a cheap point-and-shoot.

When I was learning to dive I was delighted to discover shoals of perch amongst the divers' 'props' introduced to Stoney Cove in Leicestershire. In the aircraft cockpit I have seen big perch asleep, completely immobile and oblivious to the succession of clumsy novices trailing through their home. There were also perch to be found by the *Nautilus*, a sunken mini submarine, usually smaller ones gathered around the sub's propellers. The best numbers of perch I have seen were in Bosherston Lily Pools in Pembrokeshire. Here I have seen a shoal so dense that it was almost impossible to see where it started or finished, all eyes of these hundreds of six-inch perch turned in my direction. At the other extreme I have often come across big solitary perch, often pale and battle-scarred, hiding amongst sunken trees, obviously the sole survivor of a similar tremendous shoal.

Perch shoal

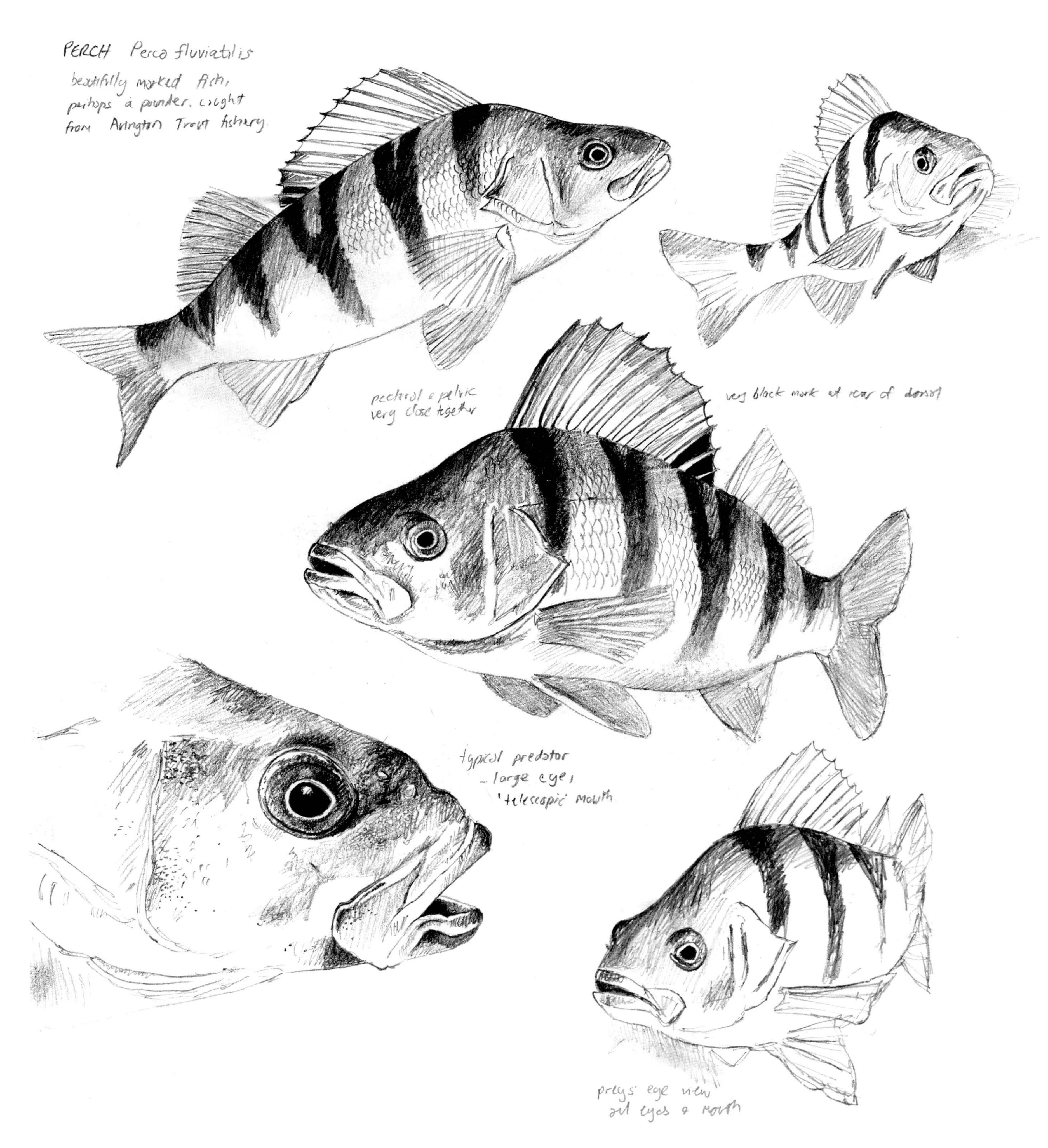
PERCH Perca fluviatilis
beautifully marked fish, perhaps a pounder, caught from Avington Trout fishery.
pectoral & pelvic very close together
very black mark at rear of dorsal
typical predator – large eye, 'telescopic' mouth
prey's eye view all eyes & mouth

PERCH AND MINNOWS

Oil on board · 12 x 16 inches

PERCH IN THE LILIES
Oil on board · 18 x 30 inches

MINNOW MAYHEM

Oil on board · 12 x 25 inches

What a splendid fish the perch is, somehow aptly described in that classic book The New Complete Angler *as 'A fish like ripe grapes'. I have seen thousands during my time as an angler and a diver, yet they never cease to delight me. I love the collective noun, I think from Bernard Venables, of 'A Swagger of Perch', for it sums up exactly how they behave, with a boldness that belies their size. In this painting I tried to imagine myself in the midst of the action as a shoal of perch attacks a shoal of minnows, a scene I have witnessed from the bank but not yet beneath the surface.*

When painting a group of fish like this, especially in water with a hint of colour, the artist is offered an excellent opportunity to create a sense of space, as the perspective is exaggerated by how quickly objects lose definition and detail. In a picture such as Minnow Mayhem *I will mix up a large amount of the background colour and block this in behind the carefully drawn fish in the foreground. I then paint the background fish wet-into-wet, which helps to create the softening effect of distance in water, and this can be exaggerated by using a fan blender to reduce contrast. This can then be taken a step further by using transparent glazes when the initial paint layer has dried, especially if a tiny amount of white is added to the pigments in the glaze.*

DAVID MILLER '03

PERCH – STONEY COVE

I can't quite believe that I haven't been back to Stoney Cove since my training dives there more than five years ago, although the delights of this flooded quarry, which include close-up views of roach, perch and pike, are offset by the fact that it is the Piccadilly Circus of the UK dive world, with 'Diver Soup' being an apt description. It is the sort of place where you can be carried away in your own little world observing the fish when suddenly a gaggle of novice divers will come crashing down on top of you. I do have plans to return soon though, especially now that I have decent camera equipment, and I am particularly keen to see if the aircraft cockpit still holds big perch.

The painting Pilot Fish *is one of my favourites in this book as I like its atmosphere and get a reminder each time I see it of my delight at finding big perch in such a setting. Thinking of perch and Stoney Cove also reminds me of my advanced training there, when I had to go deeper than I am comfortable with. I love to dive and feel completely at home underwater but not below about twenty metres. The increase in pressure and lack of light at this depth and beyond scares me and the diving ceases to be pleasurable. On one of my training dives I was down at about twenty-five metres and was starting to panic when out of the corner of my eye I saw a tiny perch and for some reason this calmed me down and I maintained control.*

THE SUBMARINER
Oil on board · 7 x 11 inches

PILOT FISH (PERCH)
Oil on board · 8 x 10 inches

Pike

Left to indulge myself I could probably paint pike forever. Of all the fish that lived long in my imagination and then overwhelmed me in reality the pike is my favourite. When I began collecting *The Fisherman's Handbook* series the pike appeared in issue 1, and even the latin name, *Esox lucius*, beside the Rod Sutterby illustration held me spellbound. For a couple of years, very much like carp, pike remained as a mythical creature only to be found in books and whispered of in anglers' tales. To my shame now, I killed the first pike I caught: I simply couldn't bare to return it, wanting to show everybody, and to somehow extend the experience by keeping it for as long as possible. I cooked the body, baking it with onions, and, much to my Mum's horror, I boiled the head in one of her saucepans trying to 'liberate the masterpiece skull'. This partly worked and I put what remained on top of the shed roof to dry in the sun, only for it to be purloined by the family tabby. I searched high and low but never found it and it bothers me to this day that I don't have that pike skull.

Rumours amongst local anglers eventually led us to Ogden Reservoir, a place whose name can still cause certain friends to swear, such a heartbreaker of a water did it become. Simply its scale was a shock to a small boy's system. I can still clearly remember clambering up to the top of the dam with Martin to gaze in awe at the twenty-seven acres (our biggest water prior to this had been a mere one and a half acres and this the largest by far of our regular haunts). We were impressed by the size of the water but were soon staggered by the size of the pike that lived there. We didn't catch any at first but we did see them: either as submarine shadows drifting off the dam wall into the depths or leaping clear of the surface, 'Like railway sleepers!' we always said. I would drift off to sleep plotting the downfall of these monsters and even wake sweating from dreams in which I had been successful.

Our early attempts on Ogden were futile due to a combination of incompetence and poor tackle. Spinning meant fishing for ten minutes until you had lost your one Mepps and your one and only Toby. Deadbaiting involved suspending a soggy sprat on a medieval snap-tackle, four feet under a Fishing Gazette Bung as big as a shipping buoy, in thirty feet of water. We even sometimes ran out of line as our local tackle shop sold a cheap brand on twenty-five-yard spools, which meant that after a couple of accidents we would be down to our wool or tape backing. The lack of success meant boredom, so sprat fights and other idiocy ensued. We persisted, even though an Ogden trip involved two bus rides and a one and a half mile walk with a creel and holdall, and eventually caught our 'railway sleepers'. My best was a fish of 22lb, not big by national standards but a local giant.

It has been with pike that I have come closest to experiencing that sixth sense that some fishermen have talked about. On a number of occasions, I have been absolutely certain that a pike is in the area I am fishing and that I should catch it within a couple of casts. This has happened both on waters I knew well and on ones I have been fishing for the first time. At Ogden, the first good fish I took from there, at 16½lb, was crystal clear in my mind as I stood on the dam wall preparing to begin sink and draw with a 4oz dead roach. I simply knew that a good fish would be hooked within a couple of casts and on the second it was. I was so sure that I felt slightly sick with apprehension and almost 'dared not cast' but stood a while with hands trembling.

Another occasion of premonition was the first time I fished Marbury Mere in Cheshire, the day after the Poet Laureate Ted Hughes had died. I love his poetry and really felt that I should catch a pike that day as a token of respect for the man and his work. I walked up to this big water knowing nothing about its depth, features or hot-spots, and felt the hairs on the back of my neck stand up as I prepared to cast. Within a second of my spoon hitting the water it was taken and a 12lb pike was soon played and landed. I have had similar experiences with other species but not nearly so often as with pike.

I now get a similar thrill from diving in pursuit of pike as I used to get when fishing for them. I have seen a lot of pike whilst diving but not yet any real monsters. They vary in their reactions to my presence more than any other species I have dived with. Some individuals drift by, apparently unconcerned, and permit a reasonably close approach, whilst others disappear at speed, often leaving a great cloud of disturbed silt behind them. In one

water that is fished regularly during the summer I have found all the marginal areas, which looked the perfect habitat, completely devoid of fish, whilst at seventy yards from the shore there were large numbers of good fish hiding in dense cover. I have often seen pike almost completely hidden in weed such as mare's tail, sometimes lying at an angle of forty-five degrees with just their heads poking up above the weed. From this position I have seen them strike at shoals of small fish passing above, so quickly that it almost makes you wonder whether the pike has moved at all. I have plans to try and photograph striking pike and have just invested in a high-speed digital SLR with housing, hoping that if I dive enough I might get some action shots.

PIKE AND RUDD

Oil on board · 24 x 36 inches

As with Out of the Blue, *this painting is as much about the prey as the predator. I really enjoyed painting these rudd, which were caught from a small pond in Hampshire and kept for a short while in a tank so I could observe them closely. I spent a long time trying to capture their characters and portray that lovely brightness of sunlight reflecting off scales. On the whole with predator/prey paintings I prefer this type of scenario, where the action is anticipated rather than in progress, which hopefully conveys an air of suspense. Any second now the pike may strike and send the shoal scattering, perhaps one rudd lighter. When observing smaller fish like rudd and roach with pike it is remarkable how close they will swim to the predator. I don't know if they have some way of knowing whether or not the pike is actively hunting or that they simply don't notice until it is too late.*

Pike, three inches long, perfect
Pike in all parts, green tigering the gold.
Killers from the egg: the malevolent aged grin.
They dance on the surface among the flies.

Or move, stunned by their own grandeur
Over a bed of emerald, silhouette
Of submarine delicacy and horror.
A hundred feet long in their world.

In ponds, under the heat-struck lily pads –
Gloom of their stillness:
Logged on last year's black leaves, watching upwards.
Or hung in an amber cavern of weeds.

The jaws' hooked clamp and fangs
Not to be changed at this date;
A life subdued to its instrument;
The gills kneading quietly, and the pectorals.

Three we kept behind glass,
Jungled in weed: three inches, four,
And four and a half: fed fry to them -
Suddenly there were two. Finally one.

PIKE AND WHITE WATER LILIES
Oil on board · 24 x 48 inches

With a sag belly and the grin it was born with.
And indeed they spare nobody.
Two, six pounds each, over two feet long,
High and dry and dead in the willow-herb –

One jammed past its gills down the other's gullet:
the outside eye stared: as a vice locks –
The same iron in this eye
Though its film shrank in death.

A pond I fished, fifty yards across,
Whose lilies and muscular tench
Had outlasted every visible stone
of the monastery that planted them –

Stilled legendary depth:
it was as deep as England. It held
Pike too immense to stir, so immense and old
That past nightfall I dared not cast

But silently cast and fished
With the hair frozen on my head
For what might move, for what eye might move
The still splashes on the dark pond,

Owls hushing the floating woods
Frail on my ear against the dream
Darkness beneath night's darkness had freed,
That rose slowly towards me, watching.

Pike by Ted Hughes

PIKE *Esox lucius*

A magnificent fish - truly "A life subdued to its instrument". An efficient predator with an almost identical forebear *Esox lepitodus* dating back 20 million years.

The business end of a small jack, with eye large relative to rest of head. This individual very pale with indistinct markings.

PIKE IN THE ROOTS

Oil on board · 12 x 18 inches

This was one of the first paintings that I had reproduced for the print market and it has, to date, been one of my most successful. It is a simple image, but one that anybody who has done any amount of pike-fishing can relate to. The fish, very typically for a pike, is lying half-hidden under cover and is studiously ignoring the angler's 'Big S' lure. The other lures hung up have sold the print time and time again, as a lost lure is a frequent occurrence when fishing near cover. They have deterred some viewers though, who have said that they would prefer everything natural, without the intimation of the angler.

Pictorially this piece is typical of my work in that it is a construct, built up from different reference sources to help me re-create the very clear picture I have in mind before I start to paint. The primary reference for the pike was a combination of aquarium shots and a caught fish for detail; the roots were taken from a riverbank and the patterns of light from a Scottish day-ticket fishery.

DAVID MILLER '01

PIKE AND ROACH

Oil on board · 20 x 30 inches

I only need to look at a snaggy corner of any pike water and a scene like this is conjured up in my mind. In this picture I wanted to create a feeling of suspense, of impending drama, as if the pike, a fish with tremendous acceleration over a short distance, will strike at any moment. It was painted without much planning but with a very clear mental picture for a guide, and the composition developed quickly and intuitively. It was initially sketched in very loosely, without any preliminary drawing, and I soon felt that lovely, but all too rare, sense of confidence arise that I was really on to something and that the picture would be a success.

Like most of my paintings it was completed in oils, a medium I love because they can be kept workable for long periods and used in glazes, which are perfect for helping to create the illusion of light underwater. After establishing all the elements very loosely I then set aside a day for working on the pike and the background wet-into-wet in one painting session. When I work in this way, often for a ten- or twelve-hour stretch, at the end of it all I have to be honest about whether the day has been a success and ruthless enough to wipe away a day's work if necessary. In this instance my day had gone well, and I was happy with the pike's character; all too often when drawing or painting pike they can end up looking as if they have been hit over the head with a shovel.

After leaving the pike and the background to dry for a few days I then started to work on the roach, trying to create a sense of space between them and the pike by painting them with more contrast and cleaner highlights. To augment this sense of space, after all the roach were in place and I was happy with their characters, I started to lay transparent glazes over the whole picture, which were then rubbed back over the roach and foreground branches. Through a combination of glazing, rubbing back and introducing brighter highlights and darker shadows I orchestrated the composition until I arrived at a picture that met approximately with the one my mind had started with.

Like a lot of artists my cash-flow situation often slows to a dribble, although, thankfully, this seems to happen less often with each year that passes. I was suffering a veritable cash-flow drought during the painting of Pike and Roach *and was therefore relieved when my landlord, also a collector of my work, fell in love with this picture on the easel and took it in lieu of the long-overdue rent.*

THE FOOD CHAIN

Oil on board · 24 x 48 inches

In this painting I wanted to suggest an atmosphere of lurking menace, of the legendary leviathan that emerges in anglers' tales wherever pike exist. My plan was to lull the viewer into thinking that the fish on the right was at the apex of this particular food chain, with the third fish coming as a shock when it is finally noticed. The painting was in the studio a long time as I kept playing with the level of contrast in the background fish, glazing her back, 'finding' her again, and so on, all the while asking my wife Lisa, our friends, fellow artists, indeed anyone who visited the studio, for their opinion. I think I eventually drove Lisa mad with my fussing about whether or not I had pitched things just right with the hidden monster as she finally said something along the lines of 'For goodness sake, the painting's fine. Sign it, get it framed and leave it alone!'

As ever, I took her advice, and it was then shown at the Pike Anglers' Club conference in 2005, where I was amazed by people's reaction. I had expected the hidden fish to fool one or two viewers but in reality it was only one or two who actually noticed her without being told she was there. This delighted me and it reinforced my feelings about this being one of the most successful paintings I have produced so far.

PIKE

Oil on board · 10 x 19 inches

Bream

Bream were the first species to drive me mad by being highly visible but seemingly uncatchable. We fished a stretch of canal called the 'Coalyard', and at certain times the water was very clear and bream could be seen patrolling up and down, looking huge compared to our usual catches. These bream would studiously ignore, or even bolt away from, our baited area. It can be hard fishing without any bites in opaque water but when you can see your float marooned above a little patch of white groundbait in splendid isolation it is enough to make you wish you had taken up golf. We did eventually learn to catch the bream, firstly by not chasing them up and down the canal and secondly by choosing our fishing times more carefully. These seemingly tackle- and bait-shy fish would take a big pinch of bread flake on a size 10 hook if you fished early in the morning or towards dusk. If you actually fished into the night they became positively easy and we soon learned that this was the case with many fish on hard-fished waters.

I was inspired to try for big hauls of bream by Jack Hayes, who had photographs of himself with large catches taken in Ireland, and I longed for similar success. I think his tales of sackfuls of groundbait thrown in 'orange-sized balls' went to my head and I tried this approach on modest-sized waters with smaller fish and probably put in enough bait to feed the fish for a month. I only ever managed, on waters like Tanner's Dam and Ogden Reservoir, hauls of one or two 'Skimmers', as smaller bream are known, and never really got to grips with the species. In fact, I did better with bream, catching them more often and to better sizes, when I started carp fishing. They loved a lot of the baits we used for carp and many a run in the middle of the night turned out to be a bream and not the longed-for carp.

OIL STUDY FOR MIDNIGHT BREAM

Oil on board · 10 x 19 inches

MIDNIGHT BREAM

Oil on board · 16 x 25 inches

Carp

I am just about old enough to remember when carp were something of a rarity and fishing for them was the preserve of the specialist. Most of the northern club waters I visited were general coarse fisheries with just the odd carp featuring in catches. It wasn't long, however, before I started to dream of carp, and by the age of twelve, catching one was probably more important to me than anything, other than catching pike. I was inspired a great deal by angling literature and read over the carp chapters of certain books again and again, my favourite being Dick Walker's *Stillwater Angling*. I can still bring to mind his dramatic description of the capture of Clarissa, the 44lb Redmire common, which held the British record for many years. I know that Redmire Pool is now considered to be a shadow of its former self but I would still love to fish there before I enter my dotage.

For at least a couple of frustrating seasons, carp constantly eluded reality and continued to exist only in my dreams. I fished with Martin, Paddy, Shaun and Mark, and although we all longed for carp our methods were too clumsy, our patience lacking or our tackle not up to the task. We used light tackle, cheap hooks and decrepit reels, which were fine for perch and gudgeon but hopelessly inadequate for the more powerful carp: so often we were left awestruck as an innocent-looking dip of the float led to a brief and spectacular battle which ended with us being 'smashed-up'. Our skill was lacking too, and although we had read about the value of the slipping clutch, for a long time its subtleties eluded us. We had it either screwed down tight, which invariably meant that a hooked carp would break us, or set so loose that the carp could reach the security of the weeds in seconds. I don't suppose that a non-fisherman could ever understand the intensity of desire attached to catching a particular fish and then the sense of shock and disappointment experienced at the moment of loss. Nearly thirty years after my early experiences with carp some particular losses still linger in my mind.

One hot summer fishing the farm-pond with Mark, I hooked a carp and played it to within an inch of the landing net he held only to feel the line go slack and watch the fish sink tantalisingly back into the depths. I blamed Mark, even though he had flooded his wellies in his efforts to reach the fish, and in a moment of blind frustration I envisaged kicking him into the pond. Thankfully I resisted, choking back tears of disappointment so as not to look a fool.

Another loss I remember particularly well didn't happen to me but to a boy of a similar age fishing the peg next to me and Martin on the farm-pond. It was a sultry June afternoon and we felt close to our first triumph after one or two near misses. Our concentration, fixed on porcupine quills cocked perfectly next to a bed of *Potamogeton*, was broken by a flurry of activity from the next swim. The boy there had obviously hooked a carp and seemed overcome with terror. He looked at us, looked back at the impressive swirl under his hooped-over rod, squealed and immediately let go of the rod as if it were on fire, taking a couple of steps back just for good measure. The rod then proceeded to rattle along the pallet the boy was sat on and disappear into the water before either of us could reach it. As he sat there, bawling over his lost rod, we thought him simply mad: to lose a carp was one thing, but to just let one go!

We did eventually catch carp – Martin first of all with a 9lb giant common from Tanner's Dam, the landing of which was celebrated with a jubilant war-dance by the lakeside. My own first was a stock fish of less than a pound from the farm-pond but I couldn't have been happier if it had been 20lb; it was kissed before being returned. We were soon catching carp regularly; in fact, within a couple of years we were at least as successful as any other carp fishermen at our regular haunts.

Night-fishing was our next great endeavour – 'doing a nighty' as we termed it – much to the horror of our parents, although at least I let mine know when I was due home. Paddy once told his mum that he was off to do an afternoon's fishing only to return two days later with the excuse: 'But Mum, I was catching.'

It was with Paddy, and mostly due to carp, that, aged fifteen, I ran away from home on the first day of our fifth year at secondary school. We had spent the long summer holidays fishing almost continually for carp, had discovered the delights of catching fish on floating crust and were starting to catch the better specimens from our local waters. The weather on that first day back at school was glorious, the bright sunshine mocking our confinement, and at morning break Paddy's eyes seemed to be elsewhere. 'Dave, let's go fishing,' he said. That was impossible I thought, but it seemed equally impossible to spend the next double lesson in the chemistry lab, and so we were soon strolling as nonchalantly as possible out of the school's back gate and into the sunshine.

We collected fishing tackle, clothes, sleeping bags and food and headed off into the wilds of Saddleworth; I think envisaging a Huckleberry Finn sort of existence. To my embarrassment now, come the evening my resolve had weakened. Thoughts of worried parents, police search parties, local headlines and all the inevitable consequences of staying away overwhelmed me, so we returned home defeated. My parents were horrified, not quite believing that I had simply wanted to go fishing, whilst Paddy's Dad laughed, 'You didn't even manage a bloody night out – call yourselves runaways!' The after-school detention was awful.

I fished more or less obsessively for carp into my early twenties but then drifted away as carp-fishing lost its mystique for me. What finished off my enthusiasm was moving on to waters where on landing a carp a neighbouring angler could wander over and, after a brief look at the fish, tell you its name and weight to within a couple of ounces. I became more interested in pike and game fish and at least as keen on painting fish as catching them. Along with his brother Shaun, Paddy went on to become very much the successful carp-angler that we had all dreamed of being, catching dozens of twenty, thirty and even the odd forty-pounder. Aged twelve we would have made a pact with the devil to catch any carp let alone a 'forty', so it has amused me over recent years to hear Paddy and Shaun refer to 'twenties' as small.

The carp paintings that I do now are as much a result of revisiting my youthful imagination as they are of direct observation. The hours and hours spent carp fishing would be filled with thoughts of carp, invariably monsters moving beneath the surface, and my paintings are an attempt to convert these mental images into paint. I do a lot of research for my carp pictures, diving southern gravel pits in search of fish, taking underwater photographs of both fish and their habitat, and visiting aquariums. So far my diving with carp has been a little disappointing as quite often suitable waters have a hint of colour, which reduces the visibility and results in the fish seen appearing somewhat ghostly. They are undoubtedly curious about my presence though and I have had some good 'twenties' investigate me before ghosting away.

Perhaps not surprisingly given their huge popularity, I have done well commercially with carp, the night-time pictures in particular selling well as prints. I hope that I have at least partly met with the imaginations of other anglers through these paintings, and while sat waiting for a run their minds are filled with pictures of great fish moving into the baited area, one of which will make a mistake and send the indicator flying.

However, as with all the subjects that I have tackled in paint, I don't feel that I have come close to what might be achieved with carp. The sheer scale of the fish, their beauty (especially an immaculate common) and the sense of mystery that still surrounds them. I will keep trying, and am beginning to work on a canvas that will have three thirty-pounders almost life size.

DAVID
MILLER '93.

SUMMER CARP

[Opposite] · oil on board · 16 x 24 inches

CARP IN THE LILIES

[Above] · oil on board · 24 x 36 inches

Looking at my painting Summer Carp *almost makes me want to dust down my old carp rods and go carp-fishing again. The thoughts of a dog biscuit or a piece of bread crust positioned carefully against the edge of a lily and that heart-stopping moment when a great fish confidently approaches...*

The Ordnance Survey map of the Welsh countryside where I live has little blue splashes dotted everywhere, often at the end of a farm track, but each one I have investigated has turned out to be an 'Instant Fishery', overstocked with silver fish and small carp. These are not the type of waters that appeal to me and I harbour naive hopes that one day I shall drive down one of these farm tracks and find something altogether different – an ancient pool, tree-girt and forgotten, stocked at the same time as Redmire but containing giants that have lain undisturbed. Some of us never stop dreaming!

THE MYTHICAL COMMON

Oil on board · 24 x 36 inches

It is hard for me to think of the carp as an introduced species as it was already an important fish in angling folklore and literature when I first started fishing. If there is one individual that is the most iconic of any fish caught in Britain then it must surely be Clarissa, the 44lb common carp caught by Richard Walker from Redmire Pool in 1952. Chris Yates, my favourite angling author, describes in his classic book Casting at the Sun, *the capture of other Redmire giants, including a fish that broke the record held by Clarissa. More intriguingly he tells of the Redmire leviathans that remained un-caught, including a fish that became known as the 'King', described by Rod Hutchinson as looking 'as big as a man'. Lots of lesser waters than Redmire seem to hold their own elusive giants, which are often common carp rather than leathers or mirrors, and these fish become the most prized in many lakes. In this painting I have represented just such a giant, a large common that only a few anglers will glimpse, whose size and beauty will fill them with awe. In my imagination I prefer to think that this fish will remain uncaught, unseen by many, and spoken of in whispers, the cause of many a sleepless night.*

CARP Cyprinus carpio.
Objects of desire for tens of thousands of anglers.
There really is such a thing as 'Carp Fever', which I suffered from for years of my youth!
Head on carp always strike me as both very oriental but also comical - with those big lips it's almost got a sort of 'Give us a kiss then!' expression.
viewed from this angle the power revealed when a carp is hooked is clear to see in the streamlined shape & huge tail.

MIDNIGHT CARP

Oil on board · 24 x 36 inches

If any of my paintings come close to meeting with the visions in my mind's eye it is the ones painted as night scenes. This painting represents a scenario I have conjured up mentally, almost as a sort of invocation, on countless nights sat waiting for a run whilst carp-fishing. I think that sense of invocation can also drive the paintings of a quarry species, as it surely did for the cave painters of Lascaux more than 17,000 years ago. The artist has the feeling that somehow painting, drawing or making some representation of a creature might lead to some success during the hunt. This painting is also fairly typical of much of my fish work in that it is an image that would be very difficult, if not impossible, to photograph, so it relies heavily on the artist's imagination for its creation. I used fish from an aquarium as models for these specimens, the lilies and surface detail came from a Scottish loch and the patterns of light on the lake bed are from a Hampshire gravel pit. It was painted with a very limited palette of titanium white, ultramarine blue and burnt sienna.

THREE KINGS

Oil on board · 24 x 36 inches

The 'kings' in this title relates to the strain of carp that these particular fish belong to, and the painting includes one of each of the three types of king carp: common, leather and mirror. These three carp were based on fish from a public aquarium, where, alongside my friend Martin, I got into trouble for taking in pellets to get the fish to feed at the surface. Once you have got good photographs in the artificial light of an aquarium there is a lot of work to be done to then portray the fish in a naturalistic setting. This involves formulating a pleasing composition, toning down the colours of the carp to match their surroundings and orchestrating the light until it appears convincing. I often approach the problem of lighting fish convincingly by under-painting them tonally and ignoring the scales, which allows you to consider the underlying form rather than becoming bogged down with surface detail. Once I am happy that the fish look to have weight and volume I then introduce colour and detail, often trying to paint a single fish in one sitting so that I can keep the paint wet and blend and soften as I go. Objects underwater lose detail, colour and contrast quickly with increasing distance from the viewer, so here I have introduced a lot more of the water's colour to the furthest fish, kept detail to a minimum and the contrast lower than in the foreground fish.

For the habitat I used photographs taken in Bosherston Lily Pools and Rooksbury Mill, creating a stage-like setting with the fish, as they often do, feeding in a gap in the lilies. Mentioning a stage-like setting reminds me of the comments of a fellow artist, David Cowdry, who couldn't stop laughing when he first saw this piece, as it reminded him of the Three Tenors in full song. Once all the elements were in place, and to some degree the picture could be considered complete, I then started to use glazes. For these I mix a tiny amount of pigment with a medium such as liquin and with a two-inch brush lay the glaze over the whole picture. Glazes can be intensified by the addition of more pigment, made more milky by the addition of white and wiped back to the painting underneath if required. Whilst a glaze is still wet, areas can be repainted with more body colour, which is an excellent technique for increasing the intensity of highlights. In this picture there are seven or eight glazes but in others I have used as many as twenty in order to re-create the atmosphere and quality of light found underwater.

CHUB IN THE ROOTS

Oil on board · 18 x 31 inches

This is the type of picture I would conjure up in my mind as I trotted a piece of bread flake down past one of the many riverside willows on the River Dane. The actual chub in the picture came from the River Test, and this shoal has been created from one fish that was caught and kept briefly in a tank for close observation. I put a bigger fish lurking in the shadows as this ties in with my experience of chub, when, quite often, after some time spent observing a shoal of three-pounders a much bigger fish will appear from out of cover before ghosting away again.

DAVID MILLER

Roach

The first wild fish other than stickleback that I saw close up was a roach. The brightness and perfection of this creature made such an impression that it was at least partly responsible for me starting to fish. Until Jack Hayes took me fishing I didn't do too well with roach, so they remained a little mysterious with just the occasional one featuring in my hauls of perch and gudgeon. Fishing with Jack, who taught me to fish finer and feed little and often with maggots, I was soon catching roach regularly, including a monster of 1¼lbs. It took me years of fishing alone to catch a bigger roach and, as with perch, I caught so many small ones that the occasional specimen looked a different species. In fact, I started to catch good roach regularly only when I started carp fishing: one of our top-secret baits was Campbell's Meat Balls, which big roach loved!

Now any fish in good condition is a joy to behold, but there is something especially attractive to me about a roach: a freshly minted look, so perfect as to be almost surreal. Fishing a dour-coloured river in deepest winter with all the colours drained from the landscape it really does seem like a form of magic to conjure up a fin-perfect, silver-bright roach from the dark water.

My best encounters with roach whilst diving have been at Stoney Cove in Leicestershire. Whilst training here it was sometimes hard for me to concentrate on what I was supposed to be doing because I was too busy looking for the roach, perch and pike that live there. Once I had passed my basic training I started taking slices of bread down with me, concealed in the pockets of my B.C.D. (buoyancy control device). By the time I had found the fish this would have turned into liquid mush, and as I opened my pockets shoals of roach, some good ones too, would gather around whilst I chuckled into my regulator. As with perch I have seen good numbers of roach in Bosherston Lily Ponds, often being stalked by the pike lurking around the sunken trees. I have looked for big roach in the Avon at Britford, but not yet been lucky. What I have seen here makes it clear why it is sometimes hard for us as anglers to get fish to take the bait: in places the river bed is literally crawling with invertebrates.

ROACH Rutilus rutilus

ROACH

Oil on board · 18 x 31 inches

I cannot understand why I haven't painted more roach as, apart from the fact that seeing one close-to was one of the catalysts for me becoming an angler, I don't know of a more pleasing fish to the eye. Perhaps the clarity of the mental picture I have of roach is so perfect that it puts me off for fear of not being able to match it. There is the added conflict between painting the fish as they appear in their habitat and wanting to paint them as they appear in the hand. I suppose the simple answer would be to paint them lying out of water in a net but this isn't generally the type of picture that inspires me as I think it is suited more to the photographer's art.

In this painting I initially painted the roach as if they were lit by an artificial light, attempting to make them too silver, so I reworked them all, toning down the colours to tie in with their surroundings and leaving only a few real highlights on the front fish. The fish in the background were painted with softer values to begin with, and then milky glazes were added to create a sense of depth and space. I used a limited palette, which features in most of my underwater pictures, of titanium white, yellow ochre, raw umber, ultramarine blue and phthalocyanine blue, with the addition of cadmium yellow and cadmium red deep for the iris and fins.

DAVID MILLER

Tench

Most of my tench paintings have been set amongst lilies as the fish and the plant are almost inseparable in my imagination: I cannot look at the edge of a lily bed without envisaging a perfectly cocked quill (red-topped, of course) with a lobworm or a couple of grains of sweetcorn laid on beneath.

My first tench was caught on a worm beneath a float, from Tanner's Dam, and ranks highly amongst any of my boyhood angling triumphs. The intended quarry, as ever, were small perch, and the float's disappearance suggested another 2oz stripey, but the strike met with a heavier, altogether more stubborn resistance. I felt sick with apprehension as I fumbled with the clutch on my Intrepid Black Prince. I remember pleading with the Fishing Gods – 'Just let me see what it is, just let me see it – please!' And when, after fraught minutes of the fish plunging heavily, I saw an oily green swirl at the surface, the pleading changed to: 'Please let me land it, let me see it, let me touch it!'

The Fishing Gods were kind and the fish (a monster of 1½ lbs) was drawn into the waiting landing net and laid reverentially on the grassy bank. The wonder then as the folds of the net revealed for the first time the exquisite creature, perfectly proportioned, so smooth and green, a green accentuated by that unlikely red eye, and set with the tiniest of scales, those big paddle-like fins, the whole a thousand times prettier than any illustration had suggested.

I went on to catch lots of tench and have retained a real soft spot for the species. One of our fishing methods (I think invented by my friend Paddy) became known as the 'Octopus' and was simply the most unfeasibly large bunch of worms that could be threaded onto a size 8, often fished free-line.

I was really disappointed with all of our boyhood tench waters in one respect though, and that was that the tench never 'bubbled'. All the text books said that they should and *Fishing with Mr Crabtree* even had a lovely line drawing of a perfectly cocked float surrounded by bubbles. I was delighted therefore whilst studying art in Wales to discover a beautiful lily-covered lake filled with fat tench where they were not only as big as my very best childhood fish but also made the water surface positively fizz with bubbles.

Tench

The cooing of doves, the hum of bees, and all the pageantry of high summer seem somehow to be recalled by the word 'tench'. Perhaps it is that this fish invites meditation. During the hours, or it may be days, that he has to wait for a bite, even the most unobservant angler can hardly fail to take note of his surroundings

And so the doves and the bees gradually compel a drowsy recognition; the wonderful lights and shades of a July noon first catch and then arrest the eye; a discovery is made that the sky glows with the blue of the south, and that the water is a marvellous and transparent brown; moreover, the insect world moves to and fro, a constant procession of unending activity, and yonder emerald green dragonfly is hovering above the crimson cork that marks the whereabouts of the angler's neglected worm ...

AN ANGLER FOR ALL SEASONS
BY H. T. SHERINGHAM

DAVID MILLER 06.

Barbel

The barbel was another childhood favourite, but it is also a fish that lived far too long only in my dreams. The fact that I had very little chance of catching barbel from any of my local waters didn't prevent me reading everything that I could on the species. Alongside bass they were probably the most dreamt-of, out-of-reach fish of my boyhood. Shortly after we had started to fish the River Dane rumours began to circulate that barbel were being caught, and even this was enough to set my heart racing and give me butterflies whenever I fished there.

To this day I haven't had my angler's dreams of barbel fulfilled, having only caught one, but I have been blessed with beginner's luck on my first serious attempt at diving with them. This was in the Hampshire Avon, where I shared a classic overhanging willow swim with a group of large barbel, many into double figures. Andy Brown of Avon Angling, who knows the river well, had kindly baited up a swim for me over a period of a few days, so when we arrived we found the water alive with barbel, drifting in and out of the shadow of a large willow, the occasional fish performing a feeding roll right over the baited area. Rarely have I kitted up in such a state of feverish anticipation and it was all I could do to stay calm enough to double-check my diving and camera kit before entering the water. When I finally did I was shocked at how cold the water was, but this was soon forgotten as the visibility was good and the prospects for great photographs very promising. I worked my way as slowly as I could bear towards the willow, trying to stay calm, keeping my breath steady so as not to send all the fish scattering up-river. Watching from the bank, Andy saw that at least half the shoal had done just that, but the remainder, as he had predicted, had sought the sanctuary of the willow.

The first I saw clearly, spotlighted in the beam of my strobe light, were a brace of large fish, looking as shocked at my arrival as I was amazed at them. When I say large, they actually looked enormous – they were clearly 'doubles', and when you bear in mind that everything viewed underwater appears magnified by 30% and that these fish were only a couple of feet away, you can imagine how impressive they appeared. The fish were not quite as relaxed as barbel apparently can be, perhaps due to the relatively shallow water, and the bulk of the shoal had pushed their way into heavy cover. This was amongst the tangle of willow roots and branches, which made photography difficult, as did the silt stirred up by such a concentration of big fish. It was simply awesome to view these beautiful creatures at such close quarters. At times, as I squeezed further under the cover, I had the flanks of double-figure fish within touching distance. After some time the fish began to settle to my presence and I chuckled into my regulator as a double-figure Hampshire Avon barbel, a fish of childhood dreams, started to feed within a foot of where I lay. I have yet to return, but I hope that this is merely the first of many such encounters. The experience, probably the best of my dives with coarse fish, meant as much to me as catching a good barbel ever could, and somehow made up for my poor efforts with the species as an angler.

The capture of my one and only barbel had a dream-like quality about it. I was fishing the River Wye for the first time, link-ledgering sweetcorn in a classic-looking swim where a gravel run dropped into deeper water under a bank-side willow. The very first cast resulted in a 4lb chub, the second a 5lb chub, the third a 6lb (and still my best ever) chub. This is madness, I thought, surely it can't get any better, but the fourth cast conjured up a fin-perfect 4lb barbel, which resulted in a little dance in the riverside field. Greedy as ever, I hoped that the barbel would increase in size with each cast but although I fished for another hour into darkness, I didn't get so much as another knock.

Barbel, River Avon

UNDER THE WILLOWS

Oil on board · 12 x 24 inches

This was painted before my experiences in the Hampshire Avon and was based again on a very clear picture I had in my mind from just thinking about fishing for barbel in such a situation. In reality the fish were much bigger, there were lots more of them and it was very dark! The models for these two were from the Blue Planet Aquarium near Chester, whilst the habitat details were from the River Usk. I had dived the Usk to watch salmon and sea-trout but having heard rumours of barbel I searched out any likely-looking swims. I did find barbel, hidden amongst boulders in one of the salmon lies, and they were the cutest fish imaginable, each a perfect miniature 'barbeling' of six inches or so. I have heard how, in some rivers, small barbel are rarely seen. This shoal was in twelve feet of water, hiding in what amounted to a small cave, and would have been impossible to spot from the bank.

[Following Spread]

AUTUMN GOLD

Oil on board · 17 x 30 inches

GAME FISH

Game Fish

I caught hundreds of trout and grayling throughout my youth, most of them falling to coarse-fishing methods on the River Tame, where I did eventually learn to fish the fly. My introduction to fly-fishing came at a time when I had fallen out of love with carp angling, mostly because of the heavily fished northern club waters I visited. To go from these pressured waters to the delights of rivers like the Wharfe at Grassington in late spring, with the cry of the curlew for company instead of the cacophony of electronic buzzers, re-ignited my love affair with angling. I had been told as a youngster by Jack McCormack, father of one of my angling companions, Neil, that once I had tried fly-fishing the appeal of everything else would fade. For all sorts of reasons I think I came to understand what he meant by this, one of the main ones being the simplicity of fishing the fly; if you have ever fished for carp with three rods, a bivvy, bed-chair, stove, cooking utensils, kitchen sink, provisions for a week and 5kg of bait, etc., then you can imagine the sense of liberation when you set out for a day's sport with nothing more than a waistcoat and a rod and reel weighing mere ounces. Another is the joy of casting, even for such a clumsy practitioner as myself, especially when a good cast puts a dry fly into the ring of a rise and a fish takes.

Then there is the whole world of the fly itself, from both an entomological perspective and the art of fly-tying, and I can well understand how some anglers become just as interested in these aspects of the sport as the fishing itself. I was taught to tie flies by my friend Clive, who had the patience to take someone as impractical as myself through the whip finish about three hundred times before I finally grasped it. I started with simple patterns like coch-y-bondu and pheasant-tail nymph and still recall the satisfaction of first taking a River Tame brown trout on a fly I had made myself. For a short time I became very enthusiastic about fly-tying but soon gave it up as I found it so absorbing that I was spending as many hours at the vice as at the easel.

My introduction to boat fishing also came about through fly-fishing, and some of my best days as an angler have been spent afloat in pursuit of wild brownies – days on beautiful waters like Ullswater, Windermere, Derwent Water and Malham Tarn. There is much pleasure to be had in simply being on the water amongst the best of the English landscape, places where the fish come as an added bonus. In fact, all of my game fishing has taken me to beautiful locations, places I would have visited without a rod simply for their character and atmosphere. These include the River Spey, the Welsh Dee, the Towy, the Test and the Lune, all of which ran through my head from childhood books and all of which were a joy to meet in reality.

I have actually dived more often with game fish than with coarse fish and have had memorable experiences with both salmon and sea-trout in rivers like the Aberdeenshire Dee and the Towy and her tributaries, and to a large extent diving in pursuit of these fish has replaced fishing for them. I derive as much satisfaction from a successful dive, seeing these magnificent creatures up close in their natural environment, as ever I did from catching them.

SALMON, RIVER SPEY
Oil on board · 24 x 36 inches

Brown Trout

My introduction to trout involved poaching for them on the River Tame with Martin. This led me to believe that they were easy fish, a species to be saved for later in the day when we had failed to catch more challenging fish like roach and bream. This idea came from fishing the Tame where it ran parallel to the Huddersfield Narrow Canal. The canal here was match fished so, at least during the daytime, the fish were hard to catch. Consequently, whilst trying to tempt a fish from here we would often sneak down to the river and set a handline and leave it to fish for itself. Invariably, after this was checked there would be a four to ten-inch brownie attached. The smaller fish were returned or put into the canal whilst the larger specimens were taken home to be eaten, after first showing them off proudly at the bus stop.

When day tickets became available on the river we started to fish there legally, but as our knowledge of fly-fishing was limited, we used all our usual coarse methods. We long-trotted with perch-bob floats, link-ledgered with a swing tip on the deep pools, quiver tipped on the faster runs and occasionally live-baited with minnows. This resulted in a fish which is still today one of the most impressive I've seen in terms of relative size. Imagine catching literally hundreds of trout, mostly 4oz or less, with the largest at 12oz, and it might give you some idea of how big a 1¾lb fish would look. This was a dark, autumn fish with a large head and sharp teeth, and appeared so big as to be almost supernatural. I was so overwhelmed, and perhaps still in shock from the epic battle, that I refused to believe the 'Little Samson' scales when my estimate of 'Four pounds at least!' proved to be a little over ambitious.

As ever a friend will always go one better. Some years on from my River Tame giant I was fishing Ogden Reservoir for pike with my friend Mark. He had a run, and as he struck, which he always did as if he meant it, the hooked fish leaped out of the water.

"It's a trout, a bloody trout!" he screamed.

"Don't be so daft, Mark. It's 3ft long," I replied.

"I'm telling you Dave, it's spotty!"

After a dour fight the fish got tangled in some submerged willows and I clambered precariously along a branch with the net, still convinced it was a pike. I could see the line hooked over some branches and as I pulled on it Mark's rod straightened and he cursed, thinking the fish was off. But as I pulled on the line a great flank, silver and spotty, rose to the surface and I bustled it into the net.

"*It is* a trout, a bloody great trout!" I screamed.

And what a trout, a ferox-type beast of nearly 12lb. Mark still hasn't shut up about that fish over twenty years later!

I did eventually become educated in the finer aspects of trout angling and now rate fly-fishing, either dry or upstream nymph, as amongst my favourite ways of taking fish. I was taught to fly-fish by my friend Clive, who, despite being a mathematician, makes a good boat partner. He taught me to cast on the River Tame, and I have spent many happy hours there fishing the fly with a little four weight, apologising to each fish caught for my misspent youth. Some of my most memorable fishing days have been spent on the English Lakes in my 16ft Canadian canoe, Dawn Hunter. It doesn't get much better than fishing the mayfly on a fine day on Ullswater, with a gentle breeze at your back and fish after fish rising to a good hatch. Lovely fish too, never big, but golden flanked with clear black spots, making a meal fit for a king if cooked on a bank-side fire only minutes after being taken. I have also loved fishing Malham Tarn in Yorkshire: not always an easy water but worth the effort, with fantastic-looking brownies, exquisitely marked and often 4lb plus. I say not an easy water but the first time Martin fished there he took two five-pounders.

In my experience, apart from with very small fish, diving with brown trout has usually been something of a disaster, as they have proved too shy and never really accepted my presence. I would have thought that being fiercely territorial they would return to where I had spooked them from and eventually settle, as sea-trout do. To get around this I have done a lot of cheating with brown trout, using a tank set up by the river to photograph captured fish.

THE ELUSIVE TROUT
Oil on board · 16 x 22 inches

Of all the species I have dived with brown trout are the most skittish, and apart from the rare occasions when a fish is in deep cover and presumably feels secure, there is no surer way to clear a trout pool than to lie in it with sub-aqua gear. However, I have discovered that by snorkelling rather than diving, especially in chalk streams like the Test and Itchen with a good flow of water and lots of weed, the trout will eventually drop back into their territory and can be observed at close quarters. What continues to amaze me when I get this opportunity is how the brown trout's colour, so striking out of the water, dissolves into the environment. I don't know if biologists have studied exactly how this works but it is remarkable to observe. I assume the trout's camouflage is created by a combination of the dorso-ventral counter-shading, colour, spots and highly reflective scales. I do know that a trout will respond quickly to a change in its environment, as a very dark trout caught from a peaty river and put into a pale bucket will very quickly start to lose its colour and if left overnight will appear positively bleached out by morning. Brown trout are also remarkable in how much they vary from water to water, more than any other species I know of, in terms of colour, markings, size and shape.

With regards to both these paintings I have made liberal use of artistic licence, by painting the trout so that they fit in with their environment but including more of the colour that you would see with a trout in the hand. The artist creates his own world and is searching for truth within that world rather than trying to hold a mirror up to nature. I think a clear illustration of what I mean by this can be seen by comparing these paintings with the photograph below. This photograph was taken in the beautiful River Itchen last summer with a wide-angle lens and the fish little more than a foot away from the camera, in water that any observer from above would have described as 'crystal-clear'.

CHALK-STREAM TROUT I

[Opposite] · oil on board · 11 x 15 inches

CHALK-STREAM TROUT II

[This page] · oil on board · 12 x 17 inches

FEROX AND CHAR

Oil on board · 18 x 31 inches

This painting was inspired by an evocative description, written by John Bailey, of a group of ferox hunting big shoals of char as they gathered to spawn. I had initially planned at least a dozen char but during my research I didn't really feel that I had got to know the species well enough to be quite so ambitious. I have since watched char in an aquarium in Galway, and having seen them close-to and taken dozens of photographs I will return to this subject again in the future.

I am indebted to fish biologist Alastair Thorne, who kindly supplied me with photographs of both ferox and char from his research into their predator/prey relationship.

DAVID MILLER '06.

SEA-TROUT BY MOONLIGHT

Oil on board · 9 x 24 inches

Over twenty years ago, when I first fished for sewin on the River Towy, this was the sort of mental image I would create as I worked my Mepps across the river. It is another painting that has met with a positive response from anglers, even though it is a scene that will never quite exist as it appears in paint. I have dived with sewin at night, and without a torch it is as pitch black as makes no difference, whilst with one the fish are separated out from their surroundings in an unnatural light.

With the freedom afforded by artistic licence, however, combined with a limited palette and my imagination, I can compose a painting that in some small way creates the illusion of sewin as they move in the river after dark. It is a great bonus if the painting then meets with the approval of fellow dreamers whose minds are also filled with images of fish.

RIVER TOWY SEWIN
Oil on board · 13 x 28 inches

I have been this close to many a specimen sewin and in this painting simply wanted to enjoy the beauty experienced in such an encounter. I chose to paint it as a night scene again, in order to reflect what fishing for these magnificent creatures is all about, but also to avoid the trap of being led by the reference material I have available instead of my imagination and feeling for the subject.

DAVID MILLER 94

BLUE WATER RAINBOWS

Oil on board · 8 x 24 inches

RAINBOW IN THE SHALLOWS –
RAINBOW TROUT
Oil on board · 17 x 17 inches

Grayling

Some of my best days fishing have been spent in pursuit of grayling, surely one of the loveliest fish in our rivers, days great not for the numbers or the size of the fish caught, but for the quality of the whole experience. They were autumn and winter days on the River Dee above Llangollen, standing chest-deep in the river, becoming absorbed by its beauty. My favourite method was the dry-fly, as the weak warmth of the afternoon sun often led to a hatch and by wading to the centre of the broad river grayling could be taken from beneath the bank-side trees. I never caught one of the giants that the Dee is famous for but had plenty of fish up to 1½lbs, although on some days, with clear blue skies, that special quality of late October light, the trees slowly shedding their leaves and the scent of the turning year infusing the air, the fishing hardly seemed to matter. I felt so moved by some of my days fishing there – the connection with the river, a link with unseen fish and the feeling that time had ceased to exist – that I tried to write poetry to evoke it all. My clumsy efforts failed to come close to any evocation of my feelings – of how the river, her fish and the pervading atmosphere seemed to hold me in their grip. Then I came across the Ted Hughes poem 'After Moonless Midnight', which is printed at the front of this book, and experienced at its best the magic of poetry in that visceral shock of connection with another, more eloquent imagination.

My introduction to grayling had come about much earlier on the River Tame, when, a couple of years after starting to fish there, they began to appear, as if my magic, in our catches. Wherever they had come from, they thrived in the Tame, and were soon averaging better weights than the trout, one or two memorable fish approaching 2lb. They soon became a favourite, especially as fishing for grayling offered another opportunity to step into the pages of my angling books, one of which (*Mr Crabtree's Fishing Gift Book*) had an article entitled 'North Country Grayling Time' and a lovely photograph of Arthur Oglesby landing a winter grayling from the River Derwent. I copied this picture again and again, and this heightened the pleasure of fishing the Tame with snow on the banks, long-trotting with a redworm under a bob-float.

Sadly, no doubt due to the periodic pollution the Tame suffered, the grayling disappeared as suddenly as they had arrived and it wasn't until years later on the Hampshire chalk-streams that I renewed my acquaintance with them.

As any grayling fisherman will tell you, compared with trout they are remarkably tolerant of a wading angler and after initially being spooked will soon take up station almost adjacent to your wader. They are equally as tolerant under the water, especially in chalk-streams like the Test and Itchen; using clumps of starwort and *Ranunculus* as cover, I have had some lovely close-up views of grayling.

North Country Grayling Time

ARTHUR OGLESBY

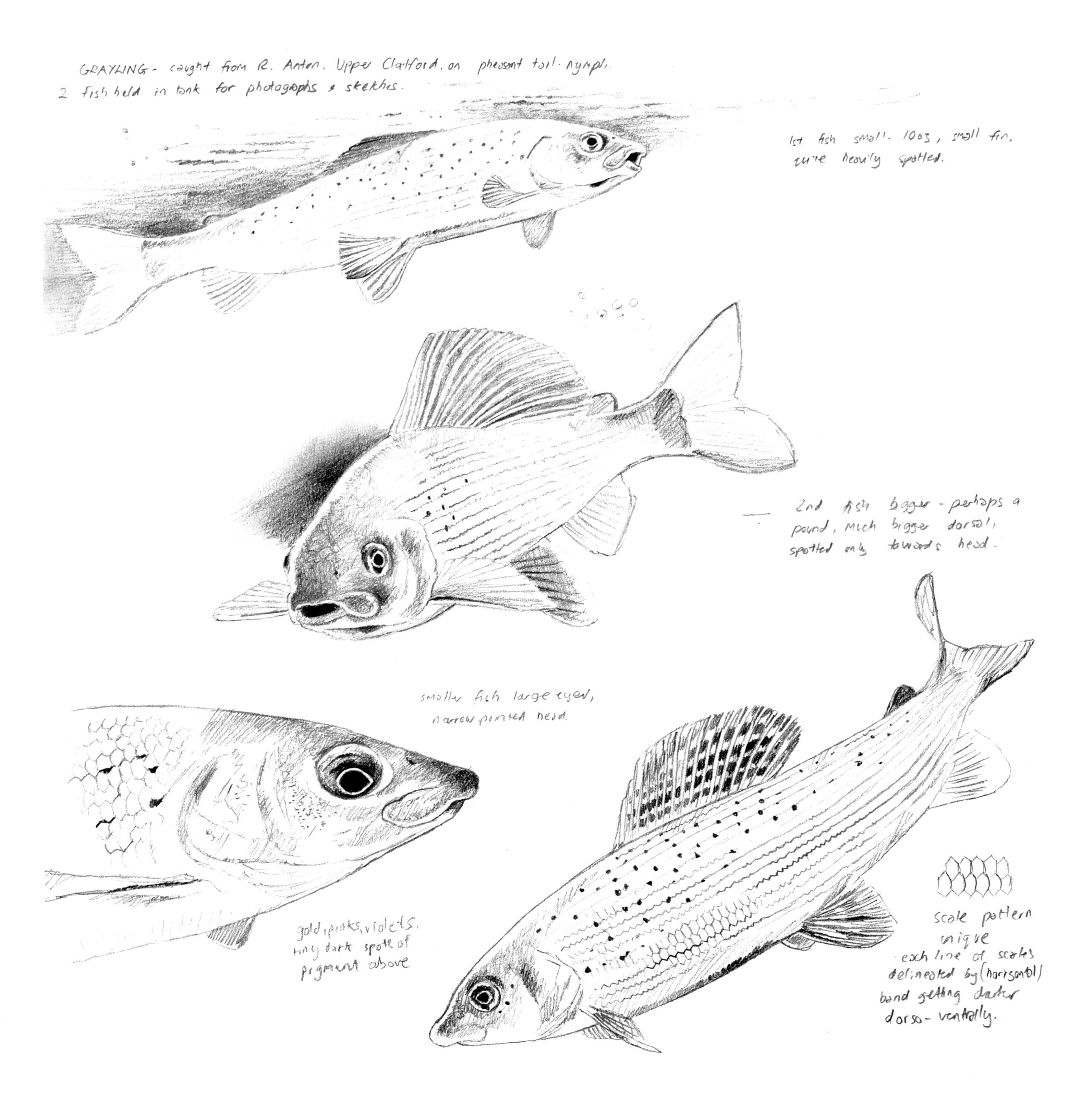
GRAYLING - caught from R. Anton. Upper Clatford, on pheasant tail nymph.
2 fish held in tank for photographs & sketches.
1st fish small. 10oz, small fin, more heavily spotted.
2nd fish bigger - perhaps a pound, much bigger dorsal, spotted only towards head.
smaller fish large eyed, narrow pointed head.
gold, pinks, violets, tiny dark spots of pigment above
scale pattern unique
each line of scales delineated by (horizontal) band getting darker dorso-ventrally.

THE LADY OF THE STREAM
Oil on board · 18 x 31 inches

DAVID MILLER '06.

AUTUMN GRAYLING

Oil on board · 12 x 20 inches

This picture is not unlike the view that can be had in chalk streams like the Test, Itchen and Anton, if you lie around in the water long enough using a clump of weed for cover and wait for the fish to return. The difference in reality would be how well the fish's camouflage works, and even at close quarters, in water that anglers would describe as 'crystal clear' or 'like tap-water' the back two fish would appear far more fugitive and ghost-like.

These fish were modelled from specimens caught in the River Anton. I am very lucky in having friends who have a stretch of this lovely river running through their garden; the water is usually clear and there are good numbers of trout and grayling present. It also happens to be just across the way from where my friend Martin now lives, so if I ever need a grayling or a brown trout as a model, a trip to the Anton will almost guarantee success. Martin has the knack of catching almost any species, on request, for the camera, and many of the stars of my paintings have fallen to his rod.

Grayling are another species that I have caught in large numbers, so I have a very clear idea of just how I want them to look in a painting, the character I am trying to portray – what birdwatchers would call 'jizz'. I often use one particular individual as a model for each fish in a painting, going so far as to copy scales and spots as accurately as I can; both are as unique to fish as fingerprints are to us. If, as an artist portraying fish, you get the scales wrong, then the fish will never look quite right. Paint too many scales and the fish looks odd because they are too small, paint too few and the opposite is true. I am lucky in this respect as I enjoy the challenge and have the patience to work on the scales until they look right, being prepared to wipe out a day's work if I have lost the plot and gone wrong at some point.

Salmon

Fishing as a small boy in a northern mill town, salmon may as well have lived on the moon, so far away and unreachable did they appear. This didn't dampen my enthusiasm, however, and I still read all the salmon chapters in my growing angling library, taking it for granted that I would one day fish for them. I copied again and again in child's watercolours the fresh-run salmon illustration by Dr Dietrich Burber from the *Collins Encyclopaedia of Fishing in the British Isles*. I also read the Reg Righyne text and loved the photograph of him in his 'beloved Lune', the idea of actually standing in the river holding strange appeal. When, some twenty years later, I did start to fish for salmon, sometimes on the Lune, at least half the fun for me was standing chest-deep in a beautiful river. I have always loved this link in angling, from literature to reality, and how satisfying it is to step into the pages of childhood books.

Most of my days salmon fishing have ended with me feeling at one with my surroundings. Repeating cast after cast, although usually without success, I have had great pleasure from the locations, fishing rivers such as the Spey, the Welsh Dee and the Lune, but have rarely experienced in angling the levels of frustration that salmon fishing can bring. To cover a pool again and again which is clearly full of salmon because they keep leaping or rolling but not get the hint of a take is enough to conjure up dark thoughts of dynamite or spear fishing.

I shouldn't complain, however, because although I have only ever caught one salmon, it did happen to be a 23-pounder. A friend, David Coates, had bought shares in a stretch of the River Usk and kindly invited me along for a day's fishing. The water was too high for the fly so we rigged up spinning rods with Tobies. We walked up river to the top pool and David pointed out a good lie on the far bank, telling me precisely where to aim my Toby. On the second cast, almost as the lure hit the water, the rod slammed over and a fish was on. Now salmon had lived for so long in my imagination and I had seen so many whilst snorkelling that to land that fish was more important to me than could be deemed rational. I knew the outfit I was using well, as I had landed lots of double-figure pike with it, so I played the fish hard, so hard that I think David was convinced that I'd lose it. I didn't and after what seemed like only seconds from it being hooked a great salmon was skilfully netted by David. As we carried the fish up the bank we were laughing like two schoolboys, awestruck by the size and power of the reddening cock-fish, which fought more in the net that it had been given chance to in the river. We hurriedly measured the fish, from which we approximated the weight later at 23lb, and then returned it, watching it swim off strongly, hopefully to complete its journey and spawn successfully.

I have still only caught that one magnificent fish but have snorkelled and dived more often with salmon than with any other species bar sea-trout. When, as a hopeful college leaver, I started to lug my portfolio and 5 × 4 transparencies around galleries I was told repeatedly that I would never sell paintings of coarse fish but had a chance with salmon and trout. This resulted in trips to Scotland to hunt for salmon in the Spey and Aberdeenshire Dee. What amazes me now is both how naive I was and how quickly I found salmon. I would simply walk the river, find what I thought to be a good-looking pool, strip down to my trunks (not even having a wet-suit for the first few trips), put on my mask and snorkel and plunge in. My one regret about those early years is not having had a decent camera, as I had a cheap Instamatic, which simply wasn't good enough. One of my most memorable experiences from those early trips was in a lovely pool on the Dee near Ballater. The pool was deep and quiet, and as I undressed not a thing stirred. I entered the river at the tail of the pool and had to fin hard to make any progress, occasionally gripping one of the huge boulders that lined the pool so as to take a breather. As the water deepened I began to see salmon, and fish after fish moved up the pool ahead of me, some clearly over 20lb. What impressed me most was the sheer strength and grace of those great fish moving effortlessly in water that threatened to sweep me away. I don't think that any painter or sculptor has yet come close to doing justice to that power and beauty. Afterwards, as I stood shivering on the shingle bank, the pool came alive, fish after fish leaping clear of the water or rolling at the surface, and I feel sure that if you had covered the fish with a fly one would have taken. I have since learned that throwing a dog into a pool was a method sometimes used to liven up docile salmon, but I've never yet heard of anyone using a wildlife artist.

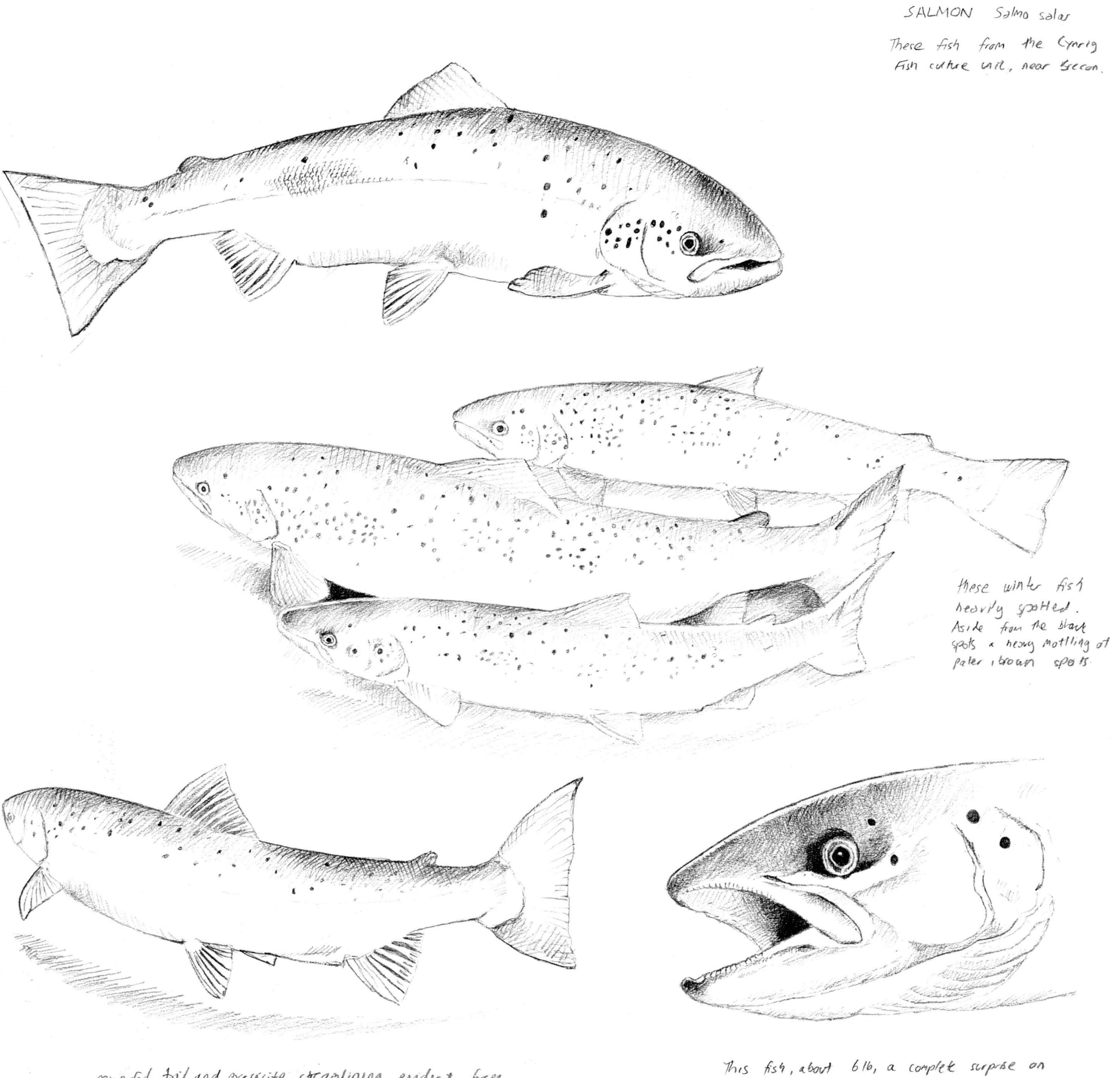
SALMON Salmo salar
These fish from the Cynrig
Fish culture unit, near Brecon.
these winter fish
heavily spotted.
Aside from the black
spots a heavy mottling of
paler, brown spots.
powerful tail and exquisite streamlining evident from
this angle.
This fish, about 6lb, a complete surprise on
Loch Awe, Boxing day, taking a Kusamo
professor intended for pike.

FRESH OFF THE TIDE –
ATLANTIC SALMON

Oil on board · 16 x 24 inches

This painting is a good example of meeting the potential viewer halfway. I mentioned in the Introduction the problems with portraying fish accurately in their environment whilst still pleasing the angler, the most likely purchaser of a piece like this.

Especially in the peat-tinged Scottish rivers, often the colour of a single malt, the freshest of fish will never appear silver but will simply mirror its surroundings; this is presumably why millions of years of evolution have made it silver in the first place. Any diver with experience of salmon in their natural habitat can appreciate this but I have found time and time again that anglers, who have their sights set on catching a fresh-run fish, expect to see this in the artist's work. So, to some extent, in this painting I have turned things on their head, by painting a fresh-run salmon and using the colours from the fish in its environment.

Ironically, after all my efforts to please an angler, the painting was bought by one of the few coracle fishermen still working on the River Towy.

RIVER SPEY SALMON

Oil on board · 24 x 36 inches

This is one of the earliest pictures in the book, painted almost ten years ago when I was still portraying salmon as they really appear ten feet beneath the surface of a Scottish river. From past experience I thought that I might struggle to find a buyer for this painting but in fact I didn't need to go any further than my framers, both non-fishermen, who loved its atmosphere and purchased it immediately, commenting on how having it on the wall would be like having an aquarium without the mess.

© DAVID MILLER '97

SEA FISH

Sea Fish

I have seen far more sea fish as a diver than I ever did as an angler. My trips in pursuit of sea fish were limited to family holidays in Cornwall and one memorable day out from Fleetwood. This was memorable not for the fish caught but for the fact that to this day I still can't quite believe that it was possible for such a small boat to survive such rough seas without sinking or that one adolescent could spend so much of a day projectile vomiting without turning his stomach inside out.

I now live only three miles from the sea and have fished my local patch occasionally, but prefer to dive whenever conditions are favourable. My favourite local sites are on the North Pembrokeshire coast, especially in late summer when the visibility is good, the water warm(ish!), and the reefs alive with shoals of sand eel and sand smelt, with bass and pollack never far away. This last summer in particular (2006) I have seen good numbers of bass, mostly schoolies of a pound or so but with the odd bigger fish. Some fish are definitely curious about a diver's presence and will actively come to investigate, but they invariably back off and even bolt out of sight from the stream of bubbles when you exhale. For this reason my closest-ever views of sea fish have been whilst snorkelling, and I have had the most success with bass and pollack by lying quietly at the surface in a likely area and waiting for the fish to come to me. I have found the best habitat to be shallow rocky gullies over sand, with a mixture of open channels and beds of kelp such as St Bride's Bay in Pembrokeshire.

One species that doesn't seem to mind the bubbles so much and reminds me in character of a saltwater version of the perch is the ballan wrasse, a fish that seems as interested in the diver as the diver is in him. I love to work my way slowly through the kelp beds, enjoying the flickering light in this other-worldly forest and watch for the wrasse that usually break cover to investigate the intruder. Seeing sea fish at such close quarters has set me wondering about developing some form of underwater angling but I have reached the conclusion that it just wouldn't be cricket! Seeing fish as regularly as I now do and noting their individual characters has changed my feelings towards them and I now rarely fish, unless it is to get close-up details of a species for reference.

The highlight of my diving so far has been off the coast of Ireland, where the waters are far richer in life than I have ever encountered off the Welsh coast. I have swam through vast shoals of sand eels and jellyfish, and every reef held hundreds of pollack and big ballan wrasse, whilst in the shallower margins each square yard seemed to be occupied by a pair of corkwing wrasse; and if I snorkelled rather than dived I saw good shoals of big mullet. Another shock in Ireland was the visibility – on my best dives it was over fifteen metres and this gives a whole new perspective on the underwater seascape.

With all of my painting I feel as though I am still serving an apprenticeship, but this is especially true of my marine work. As my underwater experiences grow so do the images presented to my mind for future paintings. I think I am like a lot of artists in hoping that I am given enough time to try and do justice to the wonders of the world that I continue to encounter.

Corkwing wrasse

opposite above Sand eel shoal, southern Ireland
opposite below Pollock, southern Ireland

[top] WRASSE IN THE KELP
Oil on block canvas · 10 x 14 inches

[above] BASS SHOAL, ST BRIDE'S BAY
Oil on block canvas · 10 x 14 inches

KINGDOM OF THE WRASSE
Oil on board · 13 x 23 inches

These are all very recent pictures, and somewhat different from the majority in this book, in that each is taken almost directly from one single experience. I have dived more than ever this last summer, visiting my local sites as often as possible and spending two weeks in Ireland.

The painting Kingdom of the Wrasse *is one of my favourites as it reminds me of a couple of my best dives to date, when I saw dozens of big wrasse amongst the kelp and hundreds of guillemots and razorbills diving for their prey. The* St Bride's Bay *picture is a typical view down one of the many sandy channels that run between the kelp beds of this popular dive site. For years I have avoided such places as I am a somewhat anti-social diver, but have discovered recently that they are popular* because *they are good spots to dive and have the benefit of easy access. This saves me having to put up with the puzzled looks of walkers and holidaymakers as I wheelbarrow my kit along a coastal path and also means that the marine life is more approachable because of its familiarity with divers.*

Bass

For many years I knew of bass only through books and magazines but they captured my imagination in a way that few other sea fish did. Why this should be so I'm not quite sure but it was the bass chapters in all my books that I returned to again and again.

As a young boy on a family holiday in Cornwall I had my first encounter with a real bass and this simply drove the species more deeply into my consciousness. I was float fishing for blennies when I saw a huge bass hunting the shallows, a fish with a back as broad as a spaniel, its great spiny dorsal fin cleaving the surface. I nearly fell off my rocky perch, dizzy with excitement, screaming at my brothers to ask if either of them had seen it.

It was not until I was in my thirties that I caught my first bass, whilst on holiday with young children of my own, and I went running back to our cottage to share the momentous news with my nonplussed family.

"Oh, that's nice dear."

Nice! It was a bass, my first-ever bass, the sea-wolf, magnificent ocean predator of storm-lashed western shores! The fact that it was only ten inches long did nothing to dampen my enthusiasm, for it was as perfect a fish as you will ever see. I have since caught lots of bass and each one reminds me of that simple joy I experienced as a boy catching a well-conditioned roach. The fish are so perfectly proportioned, the silver so bright it seems as if the light is generated from within rather than reflected off the scales.

During the summer months I dive as often as possible looking for bass, especially off the north Pembrokeshire coast. Here, amongst the kelp forests with a backdrop so blue that it appears tropical, I have seen lots of bass, some big ones too. I have enjoyed painting them as much as any other species. The painting *Bass and Sand Eels* was started almost immediately on returning to the studio after one of my first face-to-face encounters, my hair still damp and the taste of the Atlantic on my lips. This was a painting started with the brush without any preliminary drawings, quickly executed wet-into-wet with a clear mental picture of my experience as a guide. Of the queue of pictures filed away in my head for future reference the one I most want to paint is of bass, inspired by watching a large shoal feeding on mackerel. This was witnessed from a beach in Devon, but I hope that if I dive often enough I might witness a similar event beneath the surface. Whether I do or not the picture now exists and has a life of its own in my mind's eye, where I have mentally sketched out a dramatic composition of a group of large bass creating havoc amongst a shoal of panicked mackerel.

Bass, north Pembrokeshire

SEA BASS AND SAND EELS

Oil on board · 24 x 36 inches

HUNTERS IN THE KELP
Oil on canvas · 48 x 24 inches

Bass I photographed at the Silent World
aquarium, Tenby. Spiky dorsal mostly
invisible for 95% of the time - flicks up when
fish feeding or

BASS caught from the Taf estuary, Laugharne. Head very Perch like in structure, with large eye & mouth.
As with Perch, darker areas made up of tiny dots of pigmentation when viewed closely.
BASS

BASS IN THE KELP

Oil on board · 18 x 31 inches

This is a painting which, during its progress, made me thankful that I was painting in oils and not a less-forgiving medium like watercolour. I started the painting as a demonstration piece at one of the CLA Game Fairs, where I enjoyed myself immensely using a house brush to lay in the background quickly and then started the fish without any preliminary drawing. This worked well for the duration of the demonstration but once back in the studio I ran into problems, particularly with the main fish. It was an example of getting 'locked into' a fundamental flaw in the foundation of a work and proceeding against my better judgement. I persisted with the poor drawing of the main fish, particularly as I was in that strange situation of not being able to see clearly quite what was wrong with it. I often make minute adjustments, especially with heads, shaving off or adding millimetres to aspects of the drawing to try and create the character of a particular fish. Whatever I did here though, I just could not get this fish to say 'bass' clearly enough – in fact it struck me at one stage that it resembled a bizarre caricature of Eddie Izzard crossed with Julian Clary. I realised then that I had to either try and sell it for its comedy value or take drastic action. I opted for the latter and scraped the fish right back to the base colour. This meant that I could draw the fish afresh without any influence from the original character showing through, and was the course of action I should have taken much earlier. From then on completing the picture was straightforward and it has become one of my most popular images of bass to date.

BASS ON THE PLUG

Oil on board · 14 x 23 inches

This was only my third attempt at painting bass and I worked hard to get the character of the fish as I didn't feel that I had quite managed it in the first two attempts. As mentioned in the notes on Bass in the Kelp *making minute adjustments can make all the difference when drawing heads, the eyes especially being crucial in creating a likeness. All too often I find that fish look dead-eyed in paintings in a way that they never do in reality. I always work from photographs of live fish, as from the split second that a fish is killed its very essence diminishes, and this shows if an artist uses a dead specimen for a model. Apart from close attention to photographic reference I also look hard at fish that I see, both in the wild and in aquariums, and have probably caused many a nudge amongst fellow visitors to places like the Blue Planet, by standing with my nose pressed against the glass for longer than seems quite normal.*

I get completely lost when faced with a tankful of one of my favourite species, and although I am dimly aware of crowds coming and going I stand as if transfixed. My wife and children often make two or three tours of the whole aquarium whilst I stand mesmerised by the residents of the tank. I think this intense level of observation informs the mind's eye and gives you a very clear mental guide when you come to paint the species observed.

The habitat in Bass on the Plug *comes from one of my favourite dive sites, a lovely little Pembrokeshire bay where the visibility is often good and bass can be found ten yards away from the paddling holidaymakers. I can't imagine what the paddlers must think of the diver who spends half an hour in less than two feet of water being tossed around by the surf whilst taking pictures of rocks, pebbles and bubbles.*

DAVID MILLER. '03.

Mullet

Childhood impressions do count for a lot and seeing an angler fishing from the quayside in Looe Harbour with two enormous mullet laid out beside him set me longing for similar success. I fished in earnest with my handline that day and caught glimpses of grey shadows that set the heart racing. I now live near two estuaries which, at times, look like 'mullet-soup' but I have yet to catch one. My excuse is that I have not yet put much time in but what little I have has matched salmon fishing for its levels of frustration. As advised by countless authors I have fished for them on tiny Mepps, on bread and on the fly but have yet to hook a fish. In the Cleddau estuary, where I have seen phenomenal numbers of mullet, it seems at first sight that it would be harder not to catch any. Yet I have covered fish after fish with any number of fly patterns and always finished up longing for dynamite or a drift net. It has, so far, been amusing to take friends, who arrive with eyes bulging at the hoards of fish and then ask incredulously 'You haven't caught *any*...?' and then see their frustration grow as minutes turn into hours and the mullet win the day again.

The fishing has brought great pleasure though, from the joy of simply messing about in boats. I have a 16 ft Canadian canoe, and there is a real Swallows and Amazons flavour to exploring some of the creeks and pills that run into the Cleddau; finding beautiful backwaters that look as if they have never been seen by another human being, with only the cry of the curlew or redshank for company.

I have had some excellent views of mullet underwater, especially whilst snorkelling off the west coast of Ireland. I used a similar technique there to the one I use in chalkstreams for trout and grayling, which is simply to lie patiently at the surface using a patch of weed for cover and wait for the fish to come to me rather than swimming towards them. Not surprisingly, in a world where predators lurk around every corner, any hint of movement towards the fish is perceived as threatening and is treated accordingly. It can be difficult when you spot a shoal of good mullet some distance away but it always works best to curb your impatience and hope that the fish will come nearer to you as they go about their business. From an angler's point of view, mullet would be expected in harbours and estuaries, but as a diver I have often seen them off rocky coasts, including a couple of good specimens in North Haven, Skomer Island.

MULLET HAVEN

Oil on board · 12 x 19 inches

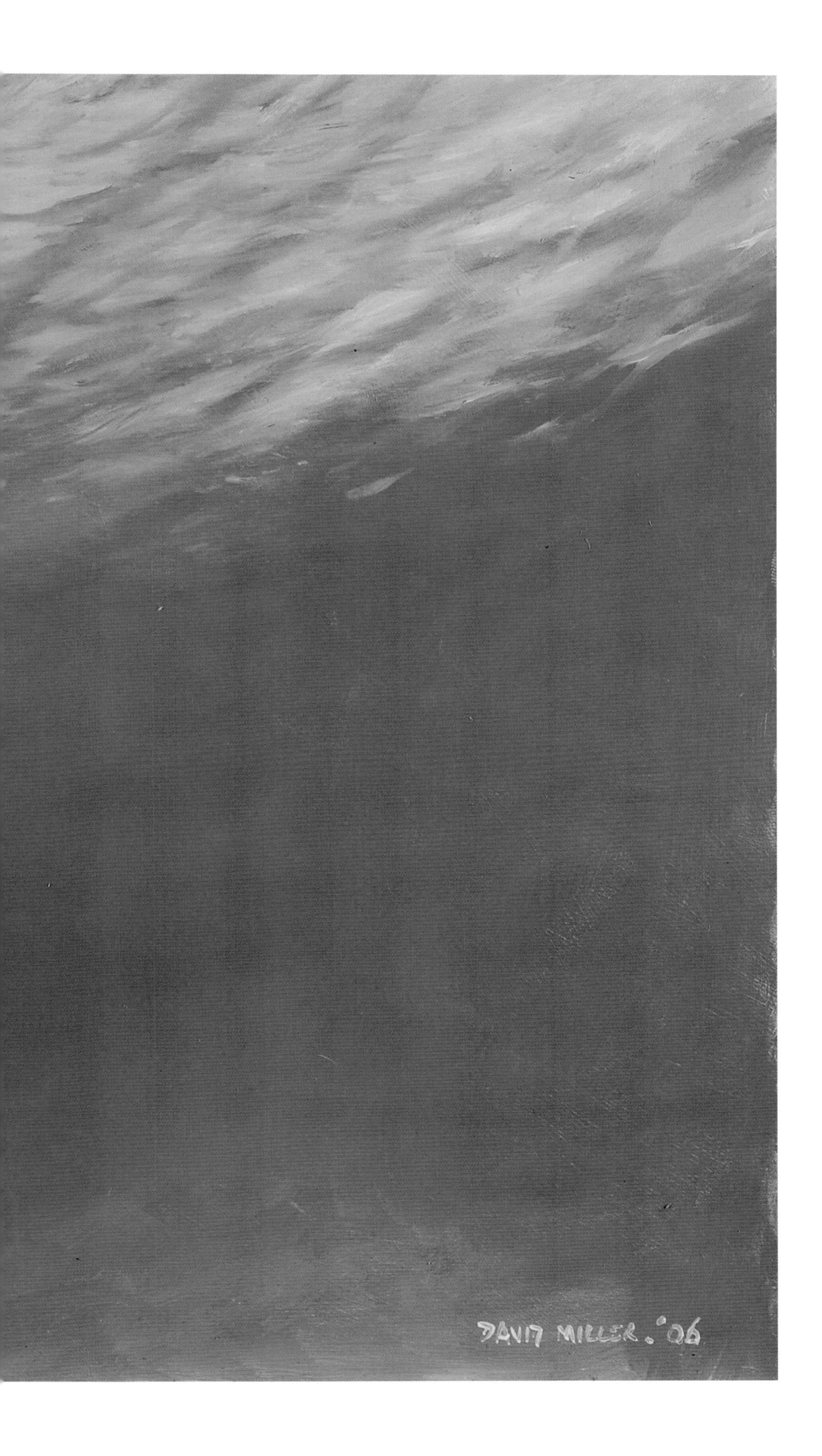

HARBOUR MULLET

Oil on board · 12 x 21 inches

At a recent exhibition I was discussing the pricing of artists' work with friends who run a Norfolk gallery and one of them commented on it all being 'smoke and mirrors'. The phrase struck a chord, because it could just as easily be applied to the artist's craft as the pricing of his work. This picture, one of my favourites in this book, is a good example. This is another image that has lived for a long time in my imagination but needed a spark from the real world to bring it into existence.

Viewing mullet in this situation from above the water I cannot help but conjure up visions of the scene beneath the surface, and mullet have swum around in my head in this sort of setting since I was a ten-year-old boy watching them shoaling beneath the fishing boats in Looe harbour. Twenty-five years later, on a training dive in Capenwray Quarry, I was looking up at a group of rainbow trout as they swam underneath the rescue boat and jetty, and the scene met with the mullet of my imagination. In the painting I changed all the colours to convey a marine harbour and used aquarium photographs for the characters of the mullet.

Further Afield

Over the past few years I have been approached by a number of United States galleries and individuals asking if I would paint certain game fish and for the most part I have politely refused. This is simply because I think the best wildlife art comes from familiarity with, and the understanding of, the chosen subject matter, and, as of yet, I have not travelled enough. The four paintings reproduced here are amongst the few exceptions that I have made to my self-imposed restrictions, and I hope that people who know these species well are not too disappointed. Each of these fish – the marlin, bonefish and tarpon – have at least swum around in my head through having made plans to fish for and dive with them. To research the paintings I used my own library of books and magazine cuttings and watched underwater footage on video and DVD. I do have plans to travel, especially as I now have a decent camera and underwater housing, and intend to start by visiting Kenya to photograph marlin, surely the most magnificent of all fish. Other foreign species that appeal to me as potential subjects include the steelhead trout, muskellunge and striped bass. Simply looking at pictures of these fish in books and magazines, and reading relevant fishing articles, has implanted their image into the store of mental pictures filed away for future reference, which reinforces how instrumental my imagination has been in all my work.

ON THE FLATS – BONEFISH
Oil on board · 17 x 25 inches

DAVID MILLER '03

MARLIN ATTACK

Oil on board · 24 x 36 inches

I have enjoyed the work of many artists who have chosen fish as their subject, some of whom are mentioned in the introduction to this book, but the only artist whose paintings leave me awestruck is Stanley Meltzoff. Whilst at college, and still searching for a way of translating my imagination into paint, a fellow student and friend, Martin Ridley, casually handed me a magazine, as he thought that the paintings in it might be of some interest. Twenty years later and I still have the relevant pages, now tatty and paint spattered, which illustrate some of the best of Meltzoff's paintings of big game fish. For me these paintings have everything that good wildlife art is all about, with their dramatic light and composition, the character of the creatures portrayed and the sublime use of oil paint. It is difficult for me not to get carried away with superlatives as I sit and look at the worn-out magazine reproductions, so I dread to think what impact the originals would have on me. All these paintings came from first-hand experience as Meltzoff dived again and again with the great fish, even once having his mask split by the spear of a marlin.

I hope to have similar experiences, although I could do without having my mask split, but until then I have studied video and DVD footage of marlin, watching the same sequences over and over again to get a feel for the subject. I created this composition quickly and intuitively, laying everything in with a broad brush, and then used details from photographs to help me complete anatomical details and portray the marlins' characters.

NIGHT OF THE SILVER KINGS – TARPON

Oil on board · 24 x 36 inches

As with the painting Ferox and Char *the inspiration for this picture came from an evocative piece of writing. This was an article in a US game-fishing magazine, which captivated me with its description of the excitement and drama involved in fishing for this incredible species after dark. To paint fish that I had never seen in the flesh I watched DVDs and referred to photographs from the huge library of images that I have built up over the last twenty years. From a technical viewpoint I find monochrome paintings easier to do, as one of the main considerations otherwise is harmonising colour and, within the course of a big painting, making thousands of decisions and minute adjustments of the palette. With monochrome paintings colour is taken out of the equation and the decisions become purely tonal. For most of my night scenes I mix up a large amount of a very dark grey, usually a combination of ultramarine blue with burnt sienna, burnt umber or raw umber. I mix up enough of this to last for the duration of the painting, keeping it fresh between sessions by either covering it with cling-film on the palette or scooping it into a plastic film canister. Mixed with titanium white, this dark grey, in effect almost black, gives me an infinite number of tones from light to dark.*

BLUE WATER TARPON

Oil on canvas 36 x 48 inches

I can't pass any of the wonderful aquariums that have sprung up around Britain in the last decade without stopping for a look. The one I visit most, as it happens to be on the route between home and family, is the Blue Planet near Chester. This is a fantastic place, although I am surprised that I haven't made my long-suffering children immune to its wonders by the sheer frequency of our visits there. Each time I go I stand in awe before the huge Carribean Reef tank and feel moved almost to tears by the sheer beauty of the scene before me. I was delighted recently when tarpon were added to the residents of this tank, as it gave me the opportunity to study up close one of the few foreign fish that have really captured my imagination. This view of the tarpon is quite similar to ones you can have there as you move through the tunnel that takes you beneath the marine tank.

I worked hard to try and portray the silver sheen on the tarpon, which really do look as if they are armour-plated. As with the bass paintings I have done, I even studied how some of the Old Masters had achieved the realistic sheen on suits of armour. I quickly realised that my early attempts had failed because I was trying hard to make everything silver when the knack seemed to be in keeping areas of maximum contrast to a minimum and in the judicious use of purest white.

© DAVID J. MILLER 05.

Glossary

ADIPOSE FIN
A small fleshy lump behind the dorsal fin on game fish.

BAIT-UP
To introduce bait into your swim in order to attract fish.

'BIG S'
A popular and successful angling lure.

BIVVY
An angler's tent.

BLOCK-IN
To quickly establish all the elements in a painting.

BODY COLOUR
Opaque paint that has the covering power to obliterate underlying colour.

BOILIES
Round, boiled and often flavoured baits used for carp fishing.

BUNG
A thick-bodied float used mainly for pike fishing.

BUZZER
(In coarse fishing) an electronic device that alerts the angler if a fish is hooked.

CHAR (ALSO SPELT CHARR)
An ancient relative of the salmon and trout. The arctic char is typically found in cold, deep northern lakes and lochs in the UK. It is the major prey fish of ferox trout.

CLUTCH
A slipping system of washers which allows strong fish to pull line off the reel before reaching the breaking strain of the line.

COARSE FISH
Typically, coarse fish do not have an adipose fin. Generally, this term applies to any freshwater fish of angling interest other than trout, salmon, char or grayling.

DEADBAITING
The use of a bought or freshly killed fish as bait for predatory fish such as pike.

DRY FLY
An artificial fly intended to float on the water surface.

DRY SUIT
A lightweight, totally waterproof diving suit; usually worn in cold weather over warm clothes.

FAN BLENDER
Fan-shaped brush used for blending colours.

FEROX
A large predatory brown trout once thought to be a separate species.

FIXED-SPOOL REEL
A reel on which the line is wrapped around a spool by a hinged metal arm known as a bale arm. The spool is 'fixed' so does not turn to recover line, although it can turn to provide a slipping drag facility.

FREE-LINE FISHING
Fishing without a float or weights on the line.

GAME FISH
Species of fish typically of the salmon family (but usually including grayling), caught for sport.

GLASS ROD
A rod made of fibreglass.

GLAZE MEDIUM
Glaze medium is a thin transparent gloss or matt coating that is applied in thin layers over another painted surface, either alone or mixed with a little pigment, to modify the original colour or tone underneath. Used in oil and acrylic painting.

GLAZE
A transparent wash of colour laid over a dry, previously painted area. Commonly used to adjust colour, value, and intensity of the underlying painting.

GROUNDBAIT
A dry mixture of breadcrumbs, crushed biscuit, crushed hemp or similar ingredients that is mixed with water and thrown into the swim to attract fish.

'INTREPID BLACK PRINCE'
A brand of fixed-spool reel.

IVAN MARKS
A leading match-angler of the 1970s and '80s.

JACK PIKE
A young pike, typically under 4lbs in weight.

'KUSAAMO PROFESSOR'
A popular and successful pike lure.

LEGERING
Fishing on the bottom of a lake or river.

LIQUIN
A quick-drying glaze medium.

LURE
Any artificial bait such as a spinner, plug or fly.

MATCH-FISHING
A competitive branch of angling in which the winner is the angler who catches the greatest weight of fish.

MDF
Medium density fibreboard.

'MEPPS'
A famous French brand of spinner.

PERCH-BOB FLOAT
A type of float often used by beginners.

PINKIE
Greenbottle maggot.

PLUG
A plastic or wooden imitation of a fish, mounted with hooks, used for catching predatory fish.

QUILL
A float made from a peacock, crow or porcupine quill.

REGULATOR
A device that allows compressed air to flow from the scuba tank to the mouth of the diver.

SCUMBLING
Dragging an opaque colour across another colour in order to produce a rough texture.

SHIPPEN
A cow shed.

SLR
Single Lens Reflex. A camera in which you view the scene through the same lens that takes the picture.

SNAP-TACKLE
Two treble hooks joined by a wire trace on to which a deadbait is mounted when fishing for pike.

SPINNER
Popular lure for almost all predatory fish. The blade is attached to a wire shaft at one end only and spins rapidly round the shaft when drawn through the water.

STRIKE
To tighten the line in order to set the hook when a fish bites, usually by raising the rod tip or lifting the rod.

SWIM
The area of water that you are fishing.

SWING TIP
A swinging arm that can be attached to the end of a rod and through which the line runs. The swing tip is lifted by the pull of a biting fish.

THUMBNAIL
Usually a small, rough sketch outlining the elements in a proposed painting.

TRACE
A length of wire used to form a particular rig.

'TOBY'
A lure used for salmon and pike fishing.

TREBLE HOOK
Three hooks joined together on to a common eye.

UNDER PAINTING
The first stage in an oil painting, using a monochrome colour as a base for composition.

WET FLY
An artificial fly intended to fish below the water surface.

WET-INTO-WET
The technique of painting wet colour into a wet surface.

WHIP FINISH
Method of completing an artificial fly.

COMPASS JELLYFISH AND PUFFIN

oil on board · 8 x 12 inches